Rural Counseling Services

by

Ramon Estrada

First published by AuthorHouse 04/14/04

ISBN: 1-4140-3613-2 (e-book)
ISBN: 1-4184-3605-4 (Paperback)

This book is printed on acid free paper.

ACKNOWLEDGMENT

Appreciation and thanks to public organizations and publishing agencies for permission of references used. Acknowledgment is hereby verified certifying that permission to references used does not include the right to grant others permission to photocopy or otherwise reproduce the reference material except for versions made by non—profit organizations for use by blind physically handicapped persons. Appreciation and thanks are hereby given to my wife for her patience and constant grammatical effort.

TABLE OF CONTENTS

PREFACE

To those who are aspiring, and to those who are counselors in rural environments, this book promotes means and ways for counseling services.

Counseling services are diversified and school population demands answers. You know theories that promote self and social healing, or as you study your population, you develop them.

Social forces and self needs intertwine seeking means of coping with each other. The stress for needed answers is the way the counselor faces counseling responsibilities.

Counseling has no theoretical solutions that solve specific self-psychological or specific social needs. You listen, you wonder, you recommend, and then you wait for desired psychological changes that will cope with self, family or social needs.

Who knows, you might have the answer for needed psychological change that may produce positive results. Counseling then becomes awareness of present existence with awareness of potential outcomes promoting deportment recommendations for tomorrow.

INTERESTING CONCEPTS OF A COUNSELOR

Always seek how, and attempt to convert
the confused thought-patterns of others.
Seek alternatives and solutions until
the feelings that have been most negative
will be conquered by your positive samples;
which then will be most developed, extracted
and implemented. They will then leave
the confused thought-patterns of others,
thinking positive and very much relieved.

Read down the last word for each line; it reads,
CONVERT OTHERS UNTIL NEGATIVE
SAMPLES EXTRACTED LEAVE OTHERS
RELIEVED.
The first letter of each word of the statement as
you spell it downwards, spells, COUNSELOR.

R. Estrada

INTRODUCTION

In 1962, in his book, <u>Toward a Psychology of Being</u>, Abraham H. Maslow wrote that the symptoms of struggle, conflict, guilt, bad conscience, anxiety, depression, frustration, tension, shame, self-punishment and feelings of inferiority or unworthiness were automatically regarded as sick and undesirable, and they should get "cured" as soon as possible. Furthermore, he wrote all of these symptoms are found in healthy people.

That was thirty-five years ago, but if you're attending college hoping to become a counselor, or if you're already a counselor today, those are precisely the major human needs that you still will face or are facing. The behavioral trials seeking solutions to alleviate self and social negative encounters are demanding major attention today.

Self and social negative behaviors are, or seem to have increased in our societal "patterns of existence" today. If these negative behaviors have increased, the question is why? Is it the social direction of our society? Is it the behavioral actions of the parents? Is it the poor quality of instruction of the educational public institutions? Could it be that all three social components mentioned have factors of failure within their systems of becoming?

If such are the social negative encounters today, solutions for the symptoms that have caused these negative encounters are needed. Expectations of such solutions for all symptoms not socially accepted are in many instances, directed toward the counselor. Pending on school systems social and academical settings, expectations will vary.

The writer, being a retired counselor, writes of his observations related to rural school systems. The following are his solutions that are not necessarily researched, but solutions implemented he found served his student-population's needs. Therefore, if you find them useful, implement them, that's the purpose of this counselor's writings.

Furthermore, the enclosed research has no scientific design knowledge; it's a three-year study conducted to seek awareness of the need, the writer feels, for "alternative education." This counselor feels "alternative education" is a dire need in our national and local educational systems.

Many night hours were spent compiling the statistics used during the three-years of the study. The results of the study confirm to this counselor what he observed during the time he provided counseling services in our public educational systems. Alternative education is a dire need whereby other means, other than total academics, should be provided to serve all the mental abilities of all student levels existing in attendance of public education.

Publication is hereby sought seeking awareness of needed future development for public educational systems. May this book serve the state and national educational agencies, school administrators, teachers, counselors, parents and future student- bodies.

The Chama Valley School Board and the Chama Valley District Superintendent providing acceptance of the three-year study are hereby commended for their awareness of the need for implementation of such needed school services. It is hoped that this school system will become an example for other school systems that are facing the same concerns.

THE SUPER-NATURAL POWER

In a democratic society such as ours, the concept of freedom for all, tends to be, at times misunderstood. Somewhere the guidance of self-development has failed to properly define the restrictions of freedom. The definition of freedom seems to have been mentally imprinted to mean, "I'm free, I can do as I wish."

Such a definition is true, but lacks its ending. One can do as one wishes in our democratic society as long as one is not imposing on the rights of others. If this ending is missing, then we would have no need for laws. The awakening of "being with total freedom" that started during the 60's seems to have caused much discord in need of self and social psychological understanding.

Comprehension of this definition of freedom should be presented to student-populations in group-counseling sessions. Furthermore, the counselees facing self and social actions that are not being accepted for the good of the social direction of their present environmental existence, should be made aware of such a definition.

Mental freedom and all behavioral actions within the mentality of any individual exists. Human beings are born with a bodily organ we call the brain. This organ has the potential to do what the individual desires and total freedom to do right or wrong. Guidance is then needed to create awareness of the difference between right and wrong as understood and accepted within the society they exist in and the consequences of both concepts.

Such guidance can be presented to groups, but this writer found it more effective when presented in individualized counseling sessions. The following is an example of the guidance approach in presenting this concept of right and wrong.

The counselor must make sure that such a presentation does not impose the counselor's views, but only those views that the counselee will be able to judge hopefully understanding the consequences of right and wrong behaviors. Carl H. Rogers presupposes this need according to Carlton E. Beck.

The counselee was referred, or the counselee referred him/herself to meet with the counselor. The reason for meeting was due to negative behaviors not accepted that were imposing on the rights of the establishment or imposition of rights to those within the establishment. After greeting and detailed information is gathered (see form at end of text), the following:

Counselor: Alright, you seem to have some problems?

Counselee: (states his views of what he/she has encountered)

Counselor: You, (states encounters). How do you feel about it?

Counselee: Well, I couldn't help it, I...

Counselor: I understand; many times we all act and do things we do not intend to do; yet, we do them. I wonder why we do so? I think we all know right from wrong but at times we don't take the time to think of actions we create, and we end up suffering the consequences. How do you feel? Do you think you were right or wrong?

Counselee: I think I was both right and wrong. I'm glad I did it, but I'm sorry I got caught.

Counselor: I guess it all depends on how you look at it, but maybe it would be better if you could make a decision one way or another. Maybe I can help you, but first let me ask you something. You don't have to answer if you don't want to, but do you belong to a religion, any religion? Just say, yes or no.

Counselee: Yes.

Counselor: Alright, let me show you this pattern I have developed. Let's go through it and maybe it'll help you.

The attached pattern provides a view and a procedure for the counselor to develop awareness of mental potential in relation to behaviors of self-actions. For the heading at the top of the pattern either the concept of "Self-Development" or the concept of "The Super-Natural Power" can be used. If the counselee belongs to a religion, the counselor becomes aware that the counselee believes in A Super-Natural Power.

The counselor presents the pattern and starts by explaining that humans have an organ, the brain that will do as the individual wishes. This organ was provided by the Super Natural Power to allow all human beings to decide for themselves how they wish to self-develop. All human beings are made aware of right and wrong by the brain, and they have the perrogative to develop themselves as they so wish.

The brain allows one to develop oneself as one desires. The individual will know actions provided are right or wrong because the brain produces that information. The individual, having been made aware of right from wrong, makes the decision as to what kind of behavior will be promoted. The decision-making mechanism is what is better know as the conscience. Your conscience promotes feelings, emotions, and releases behaviors.

Following the pattern that follows, one can see that all decisions made, whether right or wrong, carry consequences. Those consequences may be viewed as the self-development of self-pride, family honor, or social acceptance. The counselee can now understand what self-actions can do and how behaviors are major factors toward self-development. The question remains, because of our behaviors, do we feel we have promoted self- pride, family honor, and social acceptance?

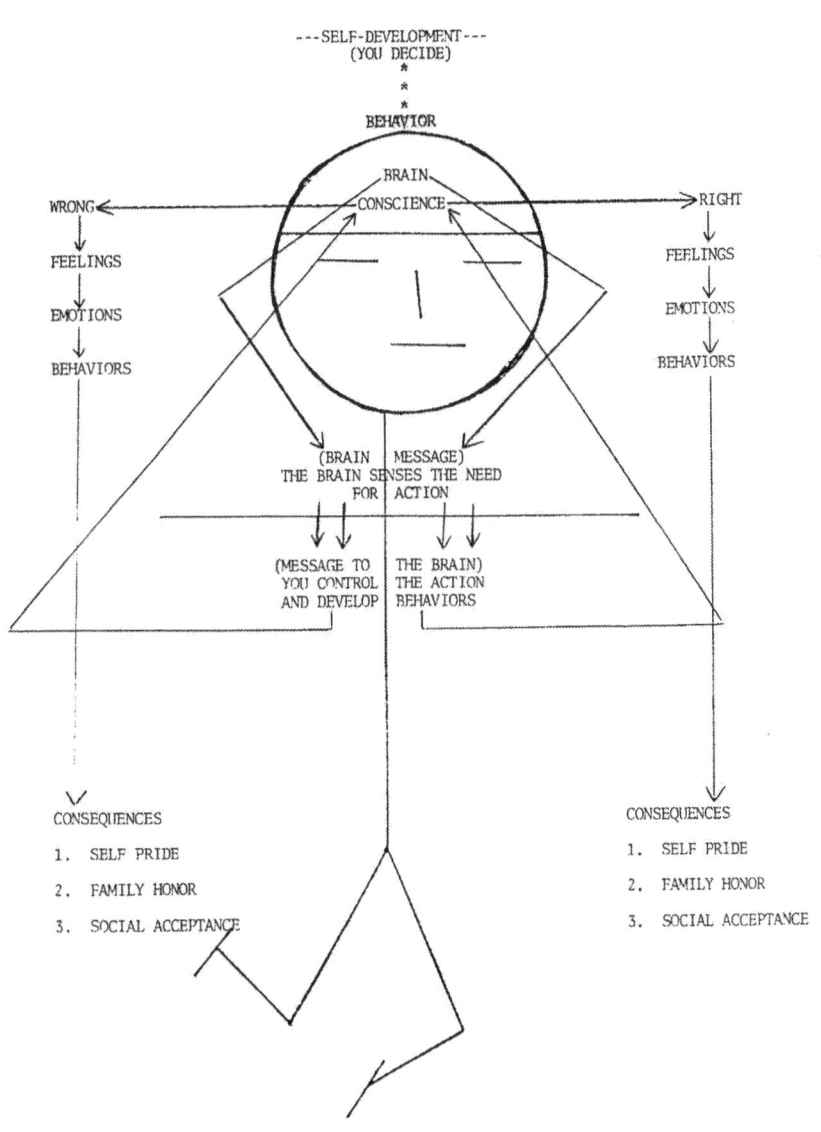

LEADERSHIP STAGES OF LIFE

Coping behaviors, as understood from readings of Donald H. Blocher, are those instrumental acts individuals perform within a social structured environment. In the social life of all individuals, at one time or another, they must become aware that leadership stages will manifest opportunities to develop their life stage of becoming. Student-populations should be made aware that social progression in life calls for them to promote leadership qualities.

During the first nine-weeks of the school year, as the counselor meets with the incoming classes, the social role model of leadership is presented. Such a developmental role model in leadership attempts to promote a series of concepts in the self-psychology of becoming.

The students are made aware of the stage in life they have reached with the understanding that each stage in life carries stronger responsibilities. Furthermore, the students are made aware that as they climb the social ladder of becoming, they must be ready to go up and down that ladder as they develop themselves. After these concepts are presented, a discussion of what leadership entails is presented.

The pattern on Leadership Stages of Life that follows, provides a conceptual presentation to assist the counselor in implementing a role-model of leadership. The stages, particularly at the elementary level should be defined. Primary grades are the start of educational development and intermediate grades are those students who no longer will be in primary grades. They are in the middle of the elementary stage preparing for mid-high.

The third-grade class is informed that they have reached the highest level of the primary grades. They are reminded of their status from kindergarten up to their present stage of education. They are made aware that they are the oldest group in the primary grades; therefore, they are the leaders.

As leaders, they must now set examples for those that follow them. Classroom, playground, and cafeteria settings are promoted as locations where they can, as leaders, set examples. A general discussion is held and they provide examples of what they will do. They are made aware that one of the greatest examples they can set is by making sure that all class work will always be finished and turned in on time.

They are reminded that they have outgrown the babyish behavior they brought to school as kindergarten students. Now they are made aware that they started from the bottom and have reached the top in a section of the body-of-education. The question then provided, "What happens to you next year?" starts the realization that life really is an "up and down" adventure.

The Leadership Stages of Life pattern is presented to them making them aware of potential cycles of life they will encounter as they develop themselves. For this age level, no further than the eighth-grade stage is recommended. This effort of social education carries much importance as they prepare themselves academically.

The fifth-graders are provided the same presentation, with of course, more maturity. They are made aware that today they reign the elementary level, but tomorrow they will be in the lowest class status at the mid-high, sixth grade, They must become aware that this stage in their lives will be a different stage in their educational development. Much emphasis at this time should be placed on true efforts of self- responsibility.

The cycle of Leadership Stages of Life at this age-level carries much more meaning for the fifth-graders. A greater understanding of the stage they have accomplished and the stage that awaits them is a major social movement for them. It is important to emphasize that there is no need for fear or tension in attendance of the mid-high. Reinforcement of the understanding that with true effort in their development, they soon will be leaders again as they become eighth-graders.

The stage of life carrying possibly the most need for change in self-awareness of being and becoming is the mid-high student population. At this stage of their lives, this age-group finds itself seeking not to be considered children and striving to be accepted as adults. Physical growth is reaching final proportions and mental growth desires to be equated in the same capacity.

The eighth-grade session on Leadership Stages of Life carries much importance. They're made aware they have reached a stage in life where they have become young adults. The counselor now requests their services on the needed leadership of the mid-high student population. Furthermore, they are made aware of the need for true samples of efforts in their academical life. They must prove their efforts as eighth-graders in order to join sports and non-academical programs.

They have reached a major cycle on the Leadership Stages of Life, and now becoming for tomorrow, depends totally on their self-efforts of today. The counselor proceeds to make them aware they are young adults today, but tomorrow in high school as freshman they must start the struggle of proving they are young adults. They'll have less difficulty in being accepted in high school if they go there knowing who they are and knowing what they want for their future development.

As the pattern of the Leadership Stages of Life is presented, they are made aware of the number of times they have had opportunities to show leadership qualities. They are made aware this will be one of the best times to prove to themselves serious efforts in promoting qualities of leadership.

This cycle of the Leadership Stages of Life for high school seniors carries a life message that their self-development efforts carry consequences. Such consequences can be mastered to degrees when they are aware that they exist. The climb on the ladder-of-life has steps that take a person to the top, and at times, to the bottom.

"And after twenty five years in the work-world, what happens?" they ask.

"You retire, and you start climbing again."

"And then, what happens?" They ask.

"I don't know, we all must die, and maybe you start climbing again!"

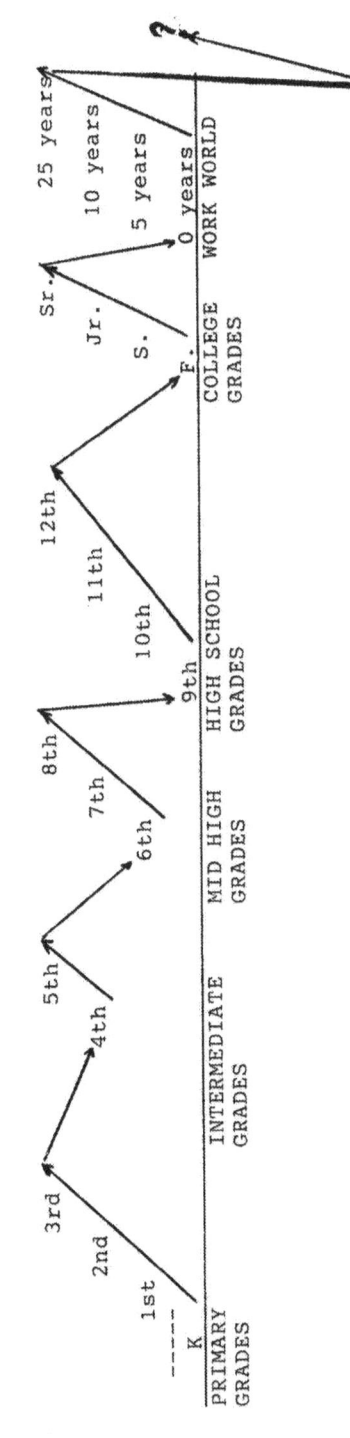

LEADERSHIP STAGES OF LIFE

JUDGEMENT THEORY

A psychosomatic behavior, which is created mostly by some form of emotional distress, is a constant extremity the counselor must confront constantly. The relationship between the mental reasoning and the physical disorder of a human being is related to what is better known as self-image.

Solutions vary toward development of self-image. Reading Gordon W. Aliport's book <u>Becoming</u>, shows that with basic considerations for a psychology of personality the view of the image at the present provides, or is in line with a view of the individual's future.

The student displaying physical disorders may well be seeking attention toward awareness of his or her being. The student is pushing, hitting others or is causing disturbances to create attention. Efforts to curb such behavior may have been applied; yet, the student has little understanding that such actions are not acceptable.

The Judgement Theory was designed to make the student aware of the needed development of self-image. The referral states the cause of the behavioral disorder. The student is made aware of the reason for the session. After pros and cons are discussed, the student is shown how the behavioral actions being created are viewed not only by staff personnel, but by all personnel in the existing environment.

The Judgement pattern that follows assists the counselor to promote the concept that all psychomotor behavioral actions are always judged by everyone at all times. All behavioral actions, whether positive or negative, are always viewed; therefore, acceptance of our being in our society depends on what actions we promote for judgement. The student is made aware that judgement is always being considered in relation to the behavior being promoted.

Also, the student must understand that negative behavior is not appreciated, and others, friends for example, hold reservations on their judgement and do not approach him or her directly. Yet, the student must understand such negative behavior is being discussed away from his or her presence.

Most students find themselves surprised that they are forever being judged at all times. The Judgement Theory presentation is an awareness of social behavioral needs that carries much effectiveness on self-image development. Such a presentation is recommended for individualized sessions.

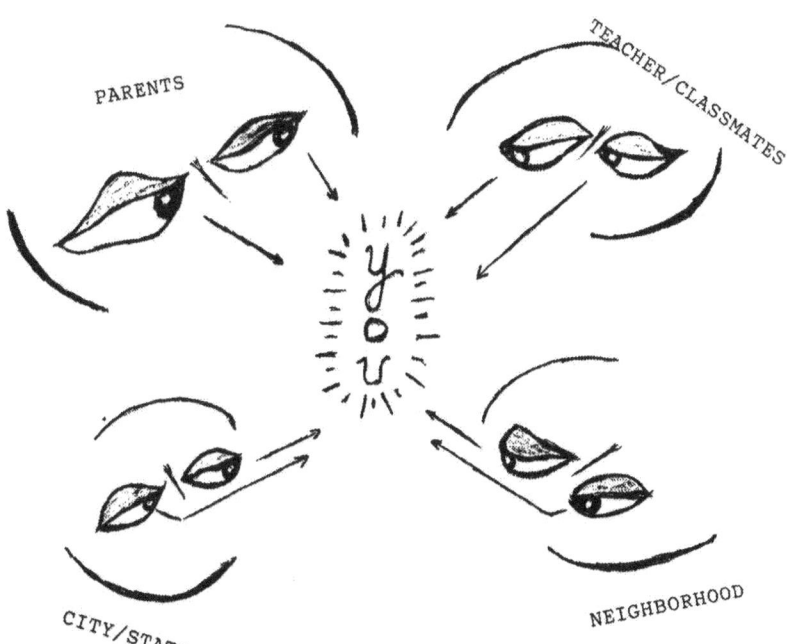

JUDGEMENT THEORY

STUDY HABIT FORMATION THEORY

Pavlov, Skinner, and Thorndike worked on the theory of conditioning and learning with dogs, cats and rats. Theorizing that the brain can form habits, the Study Habit Formation Theory attempts to condition "learning needs" of students. Such theory has proven to be effective with most students that participated. The cognitive abilities for most of them had a positive increase.

One must reason that we are a society that exists with behaviors through habits one forms. How these habits were formed depends on one's acceptance of the needs one feels are needed for one's self developmental needs. The counselor's efforts to condition a study-habit is a behavioral concept designed to develop the cognitive domain.

Experimenting with student groups from fifth to eighth grades, the following explanation of a "Study Habit Formation Theory" proved to be successful in increase and achievement of greater point average on grades. Student participation must be voluntary.

The Study Habit Formation project is implemented after the first nine-weeks of the school-year. At the end of the first nine-weeks, students get their report cards and become aware of their grades' standing. Discussion with the staff member in charge of the class prompts the need for a group counseling session. Prior to any communicative insights of the study habits review, the counselor draws a picture on the chalkboard of a baby as is portrayed in the following pages:

CHALKBOARD MODEL OF BRAIN'S EARLY "BIRTH" HABITS

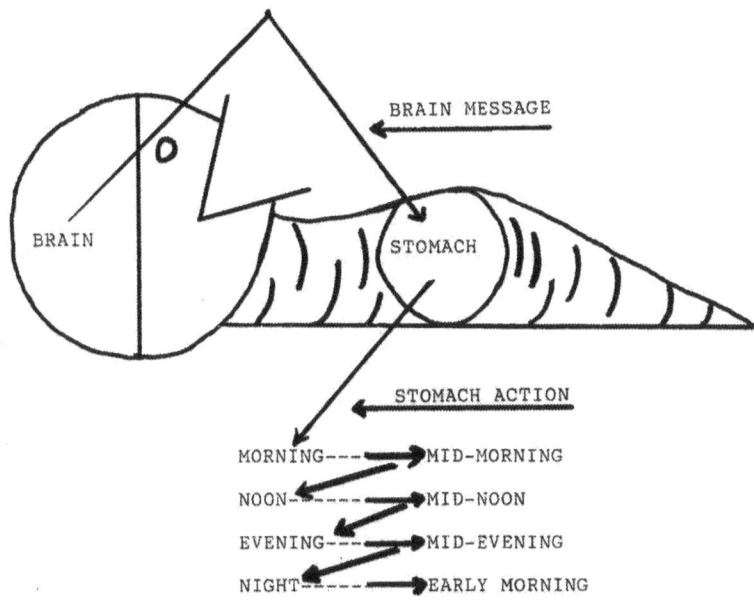

When you were born, the brain knew it had to develop you, but it had not formed any stable habits. Therefore, your stomach was forever hungry. Ask your mom; she suffered! She finally decided to form a stable habit for your confused brain.

R. Estrada, Counselor

After greetings, the counselor informs the class about the drawing that represents them as babies. The counselor addresses the class in relation to their nine-weeks's-report cards and their grades. They are informed that some of them were successful in some subject areas and some, you understand, were quite dissatisfied.

The reason, due to below-average grades, the counselor informs them, is what he's here to address. They are told that some of them may not be able to do any better. Others didn't place much effort in their studies, and still others might not know how to do better. The counselor reassures them he feels there isn't a single one of them that couldn't have done better.

The questions asked, "How many of you could have done better? How many of you will do better the second nine- weeks? How many of you will be willing to do better if I assure you that you will do better if you do as I tell you?"

After the response to these questions, the counselor tells them that after the presentation he will show them how to improve their grade-standing. The counselor makes the following statement, "Be assured, I will help you, but I only want those who are sincere and serious in wanting to improve."

The counselor starts by saying, "First of all, if you really want to improve on having better grades, you need to form a habit. This will be a habit of studying. I can see it now; you're thinking 'how can I form a habit of studying?' I know it can be done. You see, all of us live by habits that we have formed. Let me start by showing you how you formed one of the few habits you had when you were a baby.

"As a baby, you had for sure, one major habit; you wanted to survive. Your mind knew you had to be fed if you were to be developed to the person you are today. I don't know if you remember, but your mom remembers of the eating-habit you were forming. Every two or three hours you screamed for food! Twenty-four hours a day you tormented your mother, day and night. You had a lousy habit. Finally, your pale mother who had just given you birth and being quite weak, said, 'I can't take this anymore, he/she's killing me.'

"She started feeding you in the morning, at noon and in the evening. For some time she also fed you around ten or eleven o'clock at night. You cried and you screamed, but she refused to feed you at all hours of the night! What happened next? Your brain picked up the message that you were to be fed at morning, noon and evening. The brain sent the message to the stomach when to get hungry, and your crying and screaming stopped!

"That organ we call the brain sets all the habits for the behaviors of the rest of the body. The eating habit formed by the brain still exists today. Thanks to your mother for indirectly providing the brain with the knowledge that you needed to develop an eating habit. You must know, all habits formed by the brain are hard to break.

"Don't eat lunch at noon, or don't have dinner and what happens? The brain sends a message to the stomach to get hungrier; and the stomach lets you know it wants food; you hear it gurgling! You still don't feed it; then the brain reacts and sends a stronger message. The brain gives you a headache and might even make you dizzy. You eat and these symptoms go away.

"Formed habits are not easy to break. Look at the smoker; look at the drug addict; look at the alcoholic; all of them had the brain form habits for them, and now they will have a hard time breaking them. Many of them die without being able to break the habit the brain formed for them.

"Can you imagine what you would be doing today, and how you would look if the brain hadn't formed eating habits for you? You would be eating every two hours for the twenty- four hours of the day, and you can just imagine what your body would look like!

"Your brain is divided into sections that do different things. One of those sections causes the brain to receive messages that will be granted at your command. For example, place your hand on top of the desk and make a fist. That hand will not move unless you wish it to move. Wish for one of your fingers to move straight out; do it. It wouldn't have happened if you hadn't sent a message to brain to do it. All behaviors are in full control of the brain's powers. Nothing can happen without the brain; therefore, the brain can form any kind of habit that you wish."

The session is opened up to the class and many habits that have been formed are discussed. In response to questions and statements made, the counselor constantly reinforces and explains the concept that the brain formulates habits as one desires. These habits can have positive or negative results.

"The brain does not determine what is right or wrong, it knows everyone has that ability. Therefore, it formulates habits the person desires to have. Whichever habit the person feels is necessary for his or her development, the brain will develop it. The choice is yours."

When this part of the session is over, the counselor then proceeds to explain the expectations of the Study Habit Project.

"I can assist you to develop study habits, and I can assure you that your mental abilities will improve. During the next nine-weeks, if you follow what is expected, your grades will improve. Understand, once you develop study-habits, your brain will always remind you that you must spend some time daily developing yourself mentally.

"It's most important that you understand that once you develops study habits, they will always assist you as you go forward in all your future educational needs. Daily you will find yourself with the need to feed your mind with something in the academics.

"Once the Study Habit is developed, if you don't feed your mind, you will suffer the consequences. You will find out that in many instances, you will not be able to sleep. Believe me, sometimes you'll have to get up from bed and read for awhile to comply with the habit you have formed. Can you imagine yourself with a need to read or study?

"It can happen; and I'll help you develop such a habit. Again, I want to repeat what I said a few minutes ago, I want to work in this study-habit project only with students that are sincere. If you're dissatisfied with your present standing in your school work, and if you want to improve, let's do it together."

The counselor then asks for a show of hands of those who wish to be part of the project. The students wishing to participate write their name on a sheet of paper that the counselor will use for future references.

All students who are participating are informed that they will meet with the counselor the next day. Also, they are told to inform their parents that they are going to be participants of a Study Habit Project. They are informed to notify their parents that the counselor will be calling a meeting to meet with all parents of students participating.

For the students that volunteered to participate in the Study Habit Project, at the time of their meeting, a brief review of the past presentation is conducted. Be aware, students participating are students wishing to improve in their grade standing. Some of them have above average grade standing; yet, they feel they want to improve their abilities. The students are seeking means of improving in their schooling needs, and the counselor is seeking to develop their mental potential.

"I'm glad you have volunteered to develop your abilities. Such a decision on a voluntary basis shows you have reached a stage in life of what maturity is all about. When you are doing something for your own self-development without being told to do it shows that you are concerned with your behaviors as they are today. When you improve your behaviors to become a better person tomorrow, that is what maturity is all about.

"The brain is the most intelligent organ that exists in the human body. Therefore, as I have explained, it controls all our behaviors. It has developed every habit we have formed, and it never forgets to makes us aware that we wished for that habit to be formed. That's exactly what you're going to do. You're going to send a message to your brain that you wish to develop an important habit for your own self-development!

"You have to think positively; daily think that you're developing a habit of studying to better yourselves. If you think about it daily, and if you do something about its development, the study habit will develop. It's not difficult to do, but you must be committed to do it. Let me tell you how it's done.

"There's twenty-four hours in the day. Out of those twenty-four hours, you need to commit yourself to use half an hour a day to develop the study habit you wish to develop. You must do this half-an-hour a day, seven days a week. How many of you feel you can spare one-half hour every day to develop yourself? That's all you need, only one half-hour! (counselor waits for show of hands or responses)

"This half-hour that you're going to use daily must always be used at the same time; this is very important. We need to have the brain receive the message at the exact time you want to develop a study habit. After the habit is developed, the brain will send the message that you must concur with the habit you have formed.

"Once the habit is formed, the message from the brain will be sent to you daily approximately at the same time. Remember, that's why we get hungry at certain times during the day; the brain receives the message and the brain sends the message back daily.

"When, then, is the best time of the day when you will be able to spend one half-hour developing this study-habit? Remember, it's a half-hour that you're spending daily always at the same time. (counselor listens to responses, and has them write down the time they feel is the best time for them to be to totally alone for half-an-hour)

"You have written the time you'll be able to spend a half-hour developing your study habit, and of course, developing yourselves. You must, and it's very important, let your parents know at what time you need total privacy for half-an-hour.

During this half-hour, always at the same time, no music, no television, no disturbances, no friends, and no telephone calls for the next nine-weeks, half-an-hour daily; Wow! What a sacrifice you're making!

"During this half-hour you're going to study or read. Make sure you have reading material always ready; don't spend the half-hour looking for something to read. It doesn't matter what you read. Read a storybook, a magazine, a comic or even you mother's journal. Be sure that you make your brain aware that at this time for the rest of your life you will develop your mental abilities.

"Daily, during the week, this is the time you start your homework. Please don't stop after half-an-hour; continue doing it until you finish. If you finish your homework prior to the half hour, read for the remaining time. Also, if what you're reading is interesting, keep reading as long as you wish.

"Half-an-hour is a very short period of time, but it's a short length of time considering what you will gain. You're going to find out what a profit you're going to get for the rest of your life. Again, it must be done daily and always at the exact time for half-an-hour.

"Never are excuses allowed! If you're on a trip with your family, read for half-an-hour while traveling. If you're shopping, go to the car and read for half-an-hour; or sit down and read at one of the stands in the mall. Let me give you some examples of dedication to the development of the study-habit."

I was fishing one evening around six o'clock and I saw this young lady with her fishing rod and line by the river. As I approached her, I recognized her; therefore, I spoke to her, "Mary Jane, make up your mind, fish or read, you can't do both things at the same time."

"I'm not fishing right now, I'm reading for half-an- hour. Remember the study-habit formation?"

Del's father approached me one day in my office wanting to know what I was doing to his son. "Last night as we were coming from our Christmas shopping, my son asked me to turn on the interior lights of the car because he had to read. I told him that I was not turning any interior lights on. It was a bright winter night and turning the lights on could be dangerous." My wife told me, "Turn them on; he's on that study-habit project and he must read for some time."

"I turned them on, and that's why I'm here; what are you doing to my son?"

"I hope that now you're clear in what is expected. Are there any questions?

15

(counselor listens and responds to questions) Understand, all that is expected from you is true commitment to the development of yourselves. I assure you that if you do as I have told you, the only results your efforts will bring are positive ones. It has been done by others, and I know you can do it, also."

Be aware, not all participants will be able to comply with total expectations as presented. Therefore, the counselor must make adjustments on individual cases as he or she confronts them. The counselor must play the part that there are no excuses as has already been mentioned. Nevertheless, if the participant is placing true effort, excuses can be made.

The counselor reminds the students participating to discuss their views of the presentation and that a meeting with their parents will be held. Also, the form that follows is presented to the students. Once the form is completed, copies are made. Both the counselor and the participants have copies.

STUDY HABIT PROJECT

STUDENT'S NAME: _____ SCHOOL UNIT:_____

GRADE: _____ DATE.STARTED: _____DATE TO END:_____

AFTER THE STUDY-HABIT PRESENTATION, YOU HAVE DECIDED ON A VOLUNTARY BASIS TO JOIN IN THIS PROJECT THAT WILL TAKE NINE WEEKS TO COMPLETE. I'M GLAD YOU ARE WILLING TO DEVELOP YOUR MENTAL ABILITIES. IF YOU FOLLOW DIRECTIONS AS HAVE BEEN EX PLAINED, I ASSURE YOU YOUR GRADES WILL IMPROVE. IF YOU COM PLETE THE PROJECT, YOU WILL FIND OUT THIS STUDY-HABIT PROJECT WILL BE FORMED IN YOUR MIND. YOU WILL NO LONGER HAVE DIFFI CUTY STUDYING BECAUSE IT IS A HABIT YOUR MIND HAS DEVELOPED.

YOU NEED:
1. No less than half- hour of study always at the same time daily. (VERY IMPORTANT)
   A.   This study—habit project is for seven days a week. (DAILY AT THE SAME TIME)
2. You need to have reading material ready to be read during this half-hour. (ALWAYS)
   A.   Start and finish all homework even if takes longer than one-half hour.
3. During this half-hour of study, no music, no television, no disturbances, no friends' visits and no telephone calls. (TOTAL PRIVACY)
4. More than anything you need the support of your parents. (TOTAL SUPPORT)
5. Note, your commitment for the next nine-weeks will develop a life-time of self-development.

In general, per class, ten to fifteen students volunteer to join the Study Habit Project. The parents of these volunteers are then notified of their needed presence for a meeting explaining the intended services to be implemented. Depending on the "chain of command" of the school-system, the counselor proceeds to notify the parents.

The intended procedure expected of the Study Habit Project has, of course, already been discussed with the school principal and with staff personnel where the class session was held. It is recommended that the school superintendent also be notified. A copy of the memorandum sent to the parents and school administrators follows:

MEMORANDUM

To: Superintendent, School Principal and Parents
Subject: Study—Habit Project Development
From: Counselor_____
Date: _____

After the first nine-weeks grades are issued, students become aware of their grade-standing. Some of the students and some parents have some disappointments with the grade results. Students become, after these grades' disappointment, psychologically prepared for commitment toward self-development. Therefore, I'm prepared to implement a Study-Habit project that has proven successful in the past.

This Study Habit Project is a psychological implementation that forms the mental need of self-development through self study. The study attempts to eliminate constant needed "reminding" by parents and teachers of needed accomplishment of schoolwork.

Students become participants "only" on a voluntary basis. The habit-forming concept of the project demands much support from the staff and the parents.

Staff support is needed in understanding the counselor will need to meet with students that are participating. For the next nine-weeks, two or three meetings may need to be held. Individualized sessions may also be held pending on students' requests. (most group and individualized sessions take approximately thirty (30) minutes) At the end of the nine-week period of the project, success of the project's goal demands one day of total elimination of homework.

Counselor needs the support of the parents for those students that are voluntarily participating. Parents' moral support to develop the academical standing of their sons or daughters that volunteered is most important. All procedures of the Study Habit Project will be explained during the time the counselor and parents meet.

Clearance for the implementation of this project has been cleared with the district superintendent and the school principal. The counselor is implementing this project in total support of self-development for those students participating. Parents, please sign below if you will be able to attend an evening meeting in support of assisting me to help your child.

(Note: NO STUDENT IS TO ATTEND THIS MEETING, ONLY PARENTS)

The meeting will be held: School unit: _____

Date: _____ Time: _____

Please sign and check below:

PARENT (S) _____ WILL ATTEND: _____

WILL NOT ATTEND: _____

PARENTS' MEETING

For a project such as the Study Habit Development Theory, parents in general attend. Also, since the superintendent and principal have given approval, parents are interested, considering their child's grade-standing. The parents are informed of the goals and objectives of the intended project. They are made aware of their students' presentation and are provided with the same presentation.

The parents are informed that their moral support is extremely important. It is requested of them that their child be given total privacy with no disturbance for the one- half hour the child will be complying with the project.

The self-behavioral demands of the project must be reinforced by the parents. For the first three weeks, the parents need to be aware that the child is complying with being in total private surroundings daily and always at the same time.

If after a period of three weeks, the child must still be reminded, it then shows the concept desired of the project is not working as intended. Request of the parent facing this particular concern is made to either call or meet with the counselor.

The parents are informed by the counselor that as the students progress with the project, there will be times when social activities may obstruct the expected development. Request is then made of the parents to assist their child to comply with the commitment made, if at all possible.

If the child is complying with expectations of the project, the parents should compliment the child often. Also, if at all possible, the parent should visit the classroom that the child is attending. They should make the teacher aware they're interested in grade results especially since the child is now working with the Study Habit Project.

Parents should be made aware that the counselor is willing to assist them at anytime they feel there's need of either positive or negative behavioral results.

The counselor will find out parents are interested since the concept of the project is development of their child's abilities. Be prepared, as a counselor, to respond to questions. Understand the concept of habit forming and be ready to answer the general question, "Do you really believe a study-habit can be formed?"

Reassure parents it can be done. Furthermore, if any positive results are gained from this project, it will be that child's grades will improve. They have to improve; they are taking the time to study. Parents are informed that in four weeks a meeting will be held with students participating and they are welcome to attend.

REINFORCEMENT MEETING

Inform the students participating of the meeting to be held, and to bring present grades they have earned up to now. Check with the teacher or teachers on effort they have noticed for those students participating.

During this meeting, in general, the students will have positive grade results. Mention to them the views given to you from the staff. Find out if they are complying with expected time to start. Have the students discuss what they are doing. Constantly reinforce their efforts.

Make the students aware that by now they should be starting their half-hour of study without having to be re minded. Let them know that if such behavior is happening, they are on their way to develop a study habit. Reassure them that there will be a positive difference in their grade standing.

Dismiss those students that have shown success, and meet with those that are having difficulties. Most students who are meeting difficulties may be thinking they will be dismissed. On the contrary, reinforce them, and after discussion, increase your demands of expectations.

If parents attend, make sure they are given an opportunity to present their views, and as is done for the students, show your appreciation for their attendance. After all students have been dismissed, hold a general session with the parents.

STUDY HABIT TESTING RESULTS

The final four weeks of the Study Habit Project, the Counselor on a weekly basis checks with the staff on effort being applied by those participating on their class work and class assignments. The counselor has individualized sessions with students requesting to meet or with those students the teachers feel are not meeting her or his expectations. If the counselor feels there's a need for another group meeting, it should be done.

The final week of the Study Habit Project, the counselor informs the teachers of the participating students that they must not provide any homework for one day of that week. Let the teachers know that's the day the counselor will be instituting the final test. The teachers are notified that a short session of the participating group will be held to explain the home-bound test.

During the group session the counselor praises the group on their efforts toward development of a study habit. The group is made aware that now it's time to find out how successful they were in developing a study habit. They are made aware that on that particular day they will have no homework.

The participants are informed that on that day they are not to do any reading at the time they have been reading for the past nine-weeks. They are told that they are totally free of any academical responsibilities and that they may do whatever they wish to do for that day.

The counselor informs them that on that day they will find out how successful they were toward the development of a study habit. To find out, the counselor explains that's the day they will be tested. (counselor listens to reactions of students related to no homework and now a test, etc.) The test will be one that cannot be failed; it's a test they take tomorrow morning.

The test is presented to the students. They are asked to be honest with themselves and to answer truthfully. They cannot fail; therefore, only the truth is expected. The students are informed that they are to continue studying as they have done for the past nine-weeks regardless whether they have developed study habits or not. Their efforts will also show on the results of grades attained these second nine-weeks.

The following test the students take is designed to provide information on the students' behavioral efforts. One must be aware that students at this age, in general, are quite truthful. Therefore, the validity of the test and the results of the nine-weeks testing promote results of the students' efforts toward the development of a study habit.

STUDY HABIT'S TEST

PLEASE ANSWER THE FOLLOWING QUESTIONS OR MAKE THE PROPER STATEMENTS (be honest):

Student's name: _____ Grade level: _____

Date: _____

DO "NOT" READ OR STUDY ANYTHING TONIGHT. DO NOT FEED ANYTHING "ACADEMICAL" TO YOUR BRAIN TONIGHT.

1. WHAT TIME DID YOU GO TO BED?_____

2. MARK AS MANY AS NEEDED BELOW:

____A. I FELL ASLEEP RIGHT AWAY.

____B. I COULDN'T SLEEP.

____C. I GOT UP AND READ FOR A WHILE.

____D. I SLEPT WELL AFTER I READ FOR A WHILE.

____E. I COULDN'T SLEEP EVEN AFTER I READ FOR A WHILE.

____F. I FELL ASLEEP WHILE READING.

WRITE, IF YOU WISH, YOUR FEELINGS ON DEVELOPING STUDY HABITS.

_____

_____

_____

_____

BELOW AVERAGE GRADES

Staff-member:

_____

_____Nine Week's

grades

Date:_____

STUDENT'S NAME	GRADE LEVEL	LANGUAGE ARTS	SCIENCE	SOCIAL STUDIES	MATHEMATICS	VOC EDUC	MUSIC	PHYSICAL ED	DAYS ABSENT	OTHER

STUDY HABITS CONCLUSION

Formulation of a habit is psychologically a process of conditioning. The conditioning factor that develops a habit is that factor that promotes what an individual feels he or she needs. That individual's need may be either a positive or a negative need; yet, conditioning will cause a habit to be formed.

Brushing your teeth before going to bed is an example of a positive conditioning factor that developed a habit. Smoking a cigarette right after a meal is a negative conditioning factor that developed a habit. Both habits were conditioned to be developed.

The mind is an organ wishing to develop an individual as that individual wishes to be developed. It is then, or it should be then, the understanding of all individuals that self-development is totally up to each individual.

The Study Habit Project theorizes that students can be conditioned to develop a habit of study. Successful proof of this theory can only be proven when such an effort is implemented. The Study-Habit Project is a challenge for any counselor. It carries as much needed commitment for the counselor as it does for those students participating. The results have always proven to be positive. If anything, students participating were successful in their studies at least for a period of nine-weeks!

THE SUCCESS THEORY

According to Webster's <u>New World Dictionary, Second College Edition,</u> success is defined as "a favorable or satisfactory outcome or result." Successful is defined as "coming about, taking place, or turning out to be as was hoped for." Those are the definitions; so how does one acquire success in order to be successful?

What behaviors must be developed to achieve what is considered success? How does one become successful? The student, for example, that is referred due to lack of effort or because of negative behavior is not considered as being successful. The counselor is aware of the needed behaviors, try harder and behave; yet, how do you implement these needs?

The counselor's first question during the first session with the student should be, "What do you think success is?' (counselor listens to response and discusses success)

The counselor's next question should be, "Do you feel you're being successful in school?" (counselor listens to response and discusses the concept of being successful)

The counselor then mentions to the counselee that now that he or she understands what success and being successful is all about, the following designed pattern will serve to show how to be successful. The pattern, the counselor states, is a simple pattern, but it is very easy to remember, and it's the pattern that if you follow, will make you a successful person. The following Success pattern is then provided.

The counselor then asks the counselee questions related to how much effort and what kind of behavior is being provided, and who does the counselee thinks supports these actions. Below each concept stated, the counselor places either a "+" or a "—" sign based on the counselee's responses.

Rural Counseling Services

SUCCESS THEORY

EFFORT	+	BEHAVIOR	+	SUPPORT	=	SUCCESS
EFFORT IS (-)		BEHAVIOR IS (-)		SUPPORT IS (-)		SUCCESS IS (-)
EFFORT IS (-)		BEHAVIOR IS (+)		SUPPORT IS (pending)		SUCCESS IS (pending)
EFFORT IS (+)		BEHAVIOR IS (-)		SUPPORT IS (pending)		SUCCESS IS (pending)
EFFORT IS (+)		BEHAVIOR IS (+)		SUPPORT IS (+)		SUCCESS IS (+)

The counselor then explains the pattern's results as follow: Briefly the counselor shows the counselee that effort plus behavior create support for success. You have shown "effort" in attempting to further develop yourself, but your behavior is hurting you. Therefore, the class as well as the teacher will not support you. Your classmates may not tell you anything about your behavior, but I can assure you, they don't care for it. If you don't have support, you're missing out on being successful.

The same approach is provided when the counselee has a minus sign on effort and a plus on behavior. The counselor then explains that the counselee

26

has won most of the battle if behavior is a plus. Yet, the counselor states, "Every one appreciates and respects you for your behavior, but you need to prove that you really care and are trying your best. You will find out that due to your good behavior, your classmates and your teacher might feel sorry for you because they like you, but they wonder why you are not trying. They can not support you."

"The answer is very simple," the counselor points out, "you place effort on attempting to develop yourself; you develop good behavior and you will find support. Once you have that support, you'll find out it's not hard to be successful."

The Success Theory works well for group sessions. Those that are failing in any of the stated concepts become aware of their faults since eye-judgement of some classmates points them out. The success theory could be the needed outlet for any counselee to find the faults that are needed for his or her own self-development.

THREE-YEAR STUDY

CAREER-EDUCATION MAKING SYSTEM INTEREST ANALYSIS

VS

CTBS TESTING RESULTS

In most school districts counselors are assigned the duty of test coordinators. Expectations of standardized testing carry much responsibility. Pending on the school districts' location and size, expectations vary. Counselors in rural school systems find themselves, in general, with full responsibilities of testing coordination.

This counselor was the test coordinator from kindergarten to the eighth-grade in a rural school district. For the three-year period of the study, 1984/85, 1985/86 and 1986/87, two eighth-grade groups were used.

The comparative analysis that follows was designed from results of test forms of standardized tests. The standardized forms used were from the Comprehensive Tests of Basic Skills, Form U and V Norms Book Grades 7—12, Comprehensive Tests of Basic Skills Preliminary Technical Report CTBS/McGraw Hill, Inc. and the booklet, which is not a test, Career Decision—Making System, Thomas F. Harrington, Phd. and Arthur J. O'Shea, Phd..

Results were accrued for this study showing group nation al percentile per norm scales' tables acquired during the period of the study. The study does not claim scientific results' validity. The study sought a comparative analysis showing the quality of education that could promote greater interests in our school-systems.

The Three-Year Study comprised a total of one-hundred sixty-six (166) eighth-graders, eighty-two (82) females, eighty-four (84) males, one-hundred thirty-eight (138) Spanish and twenty-eight (28) Anglos. (see Form attached, 3YSP or 3-year Study Project)

The researcher and counselor of this study theorizes that our school-systems would advance the student-population's development in the cognitive, affective and psychomotor variables of the behavioral dimensions if a two-track education

28

system would be contrived to be oriented in academics and career instruction.

It seems a two-track education system is a far-fetched desire considering presumed financial factors and parental awareness of need for change. Considering financial factors, one is looking to more teachers, buildings and equipment for its development. Considering change for social dissemination for established academical patterns existing in our school systems may not be acceptable to many parents.

Such factors as mentioned would provide significant major needs toward the psychological and social development of student populations. Need for such change in our school systems can start to develop by implementation of alternative education.

Alternative education may well start in a school system with the present staff that is certified in their areas of instruction. In the areas of certification, language arts, mathematics, science, plus other instructional fields, the present staff can instruct in relation to career fields of interest to their students. Such an approach would have to take into consideration some individualized attention and the grading system.

If students are showing poor progress in academics in their standardized tests, they may be motivated to promote greater interest in effort if provided with an alternative method of showing progress. Students would be informed that they would be graded on effort as well as academic results.

For example, if in the language-arts field, they were asked to research and write about a career that interests them, they would find themselves finding procedures of attaining a career desire. Furthermore, they would be finding out what the expectations of such a career may be.

Take a student that is interested in barbering. That student would find out that oral and written communication is important to barbering. Conversational needs of barbers relate to understanding psychological approaches. One cannot by-pass the need for mathematics and awareness of the scientific expectations for control of hair growth and hair roots' treatment, etc.

Students would be graded, as mentioned, on their efforts and academical results. The staff must be made aware that if effort was placed in accomplishment of assignments, the students are to receive grades that would be no less than a "C".

The established grading system, A to F for students that are not academically oriented becomes a punishment and results to psychologically develop them as failures. If twelve- years' schooling efforts in academics show they're failures, they may well leave school to join the adult world with a failing attitude. An alternative instruction program may well be the answer toward the development of the students' future psychological and social development.

Depending on the size of the school-systems' student- population, one or two extra teachers could be hired to assist students in need of alternative instruction. The effort would promote needed instructional services and would start the efforts of a two-track educational system.

Alternative education would start with the objective of providing interest and academic instruction to students that have shown through standardized testing that they are not academically oriented. Furthermore, such instructive procedures may well serve other students that are academically oriented, but lack interest in schooling efforts. Some students, if properly tested, may prove that even though they are academically oriented, they show potential in interests related to specific careers other than careers mandating academics.

The following graphs structured from testing results for a period of three years are hereby presented. The intent of the graphs is to show the need for change in our public school systems. They are hereby presented as a comparative view showing need that should be further explored toward future expectations of school systems in their instructional patterns.

THREE YEAR STUDY

GROUP INFORMATION

The Three-Year Study, Form 3YSP, provides the following information:
1. THE THREE-YEAR STUDY POPULATION provides yearly information for the three years the study was conducted. It shows the sex and ethnicity and the total number of eighth- graders that participated.
2. TOTAL THREE-YEAR POPULATION, provides the total number of participants showing sex and ethnicity.
3. NUMBER OF STUDENTS WITH TOP SCORES IN THE DIFFERENT CATEGORIES provides by sex and ethnicity the number of students scoring high in the different career categories during the three years of the study. (Career Decision-Making System)
4. PERCENTAGE OF STUDENTS WITH HIGH SCORES IN THE DIFFERENT CATEGORIES shows total percentage of participants per category.
5. PERCENTAGE BREAKDOWN, TO THE NEAREST TENTH, OF STUDENTS' POPULATION PER CATEGORIES OF TOP SCORES, provides the highest percentage of students, by sex and ethnicity that obtained the highest scores in the different categories of careers' categories used in the study.

THREE YEAR STUDY
FORM 3YSP

THE THREE YEAR STUDY POPULATION

1984/85				1985/86				1986/87			
FEMALE	MALE	SPANISH	ANGLO	FEMALE	MALE	SPANISH	ANGLO	FEMALE	MALE	SPANISH	ANGLO
27	36	54	9	30	29	48	11	25	19	36	8

TOTAL THREE-YEAR POPULATION:

FEMALE	MALE	SPANISH	ANGLO
27	36	54	9
30	29	48	11
25	19	36	8
82	84	138	28 ---166 students

FEMALE--(F), MALE--(M), SPANISH--(S), ANGLO--(A)

NUMBER OF STUDENTS WITH TOP SCORES IN THE DIFFERENT CAREER CATEGORIES, CAREER EDUCATION SYSTEM:

THE ARTS

F	M	S	A
8	3	8	3
4	0	3	1
5	0	5	0
17	3	16	4

20 students

BUSINESS

F	M	S	A
3	3	6	0
2	2	0	0
2	0	5	1
7	5	11	1

12 students

CLERICAL

F	M	S	A
5	0	5	0
13	1	10	4
5	0	5	0
23	1	20	4

24 students

CRAFTS

F	M	S	A
0	26	22	4
1	26	25	2
0	10	8	2
1	62	55	8

63 students

SCIENTIFIC

F	M	S	A
4	4	8	0
4	2	4	2
4	5	5	4
12	11	17	6

23 students

SOCIAL

F	M	S	A	
7	0	5	2	-1984/85
6	0	4	2	-1985/86
9	2	10	1	-1986/87
22	2	19	5	

24 students--Total

PERCENTAGE BREAKDOWN, TO THE NEAREST TENTH, OF THE NUMBER OF STUDENTS' PER CATEGORIES OF TOP SCORES

THE ARTS	BUSINESS	CLERICAL	CRAFTS	SCIENTIFIC	SOCIAL
F--21.0%	F--9.0%	F--28.0%	F-- 1.0%	F--15.0%	F--27.0%
M-- 4.0%	M--6.0%	M-- 1.0%	M--74.0%	M--13.0%	M-- 2.0%
S--12.0%	S--8.0%	S--14.0%	S--40.0%	S--12.0%	S--14.0%
A--14.0%	A--4.0%	A--14.0%	A--29.0%	A--21.0%	A--18.0%

GROUP PERCENTAGE OF THE NUMBER STUDENTS WITH HIGH SCORES IN THE DIFFERENT CAREER CATEGORIES

THE ARTS	BUSINESS	CLERICAL	CRAFTS	SCIENTIFIC	SOCIAL
12%	7.2%	14.5%	37.9%	13.8%	14.5%

31

PERCENTAGE OF STUDENTS WITH HIGH SCORES

THREE-YEAR STUDY

The pie graph shows the total number of students and the percentage of total student-group in the study that attained highest marks in the six different career categories.

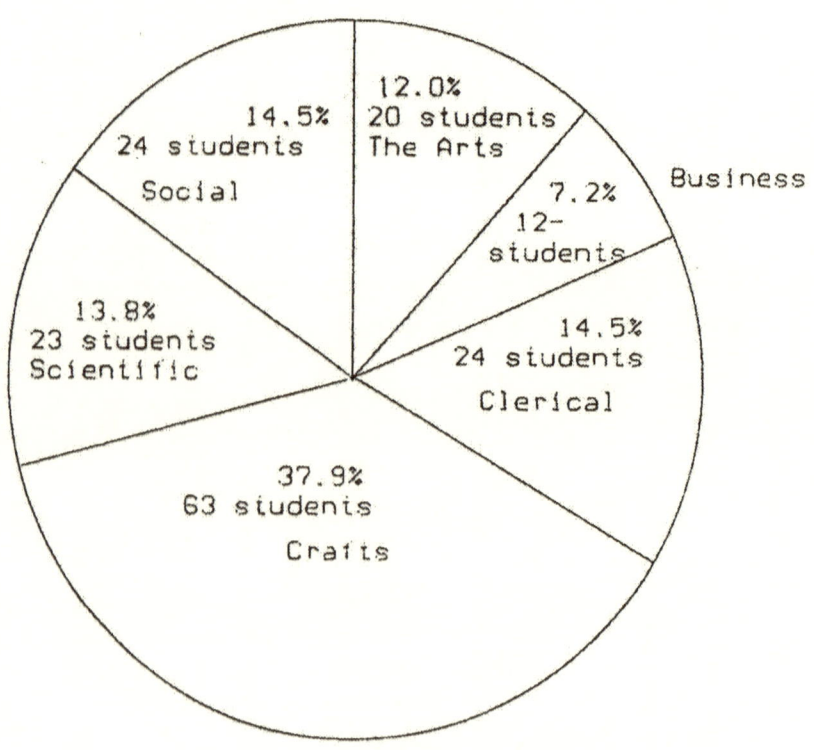

PERCENTAGE OF STUDENTS WITH HIGH SCORES
THREE-YEAR STUDY

SPANISH/ANGLO

CAREER DECISION CATEGORIES

The pie graph shows the number of students and percentage of ethnicity divisions attaining high scores in the six career categories of the three year study.

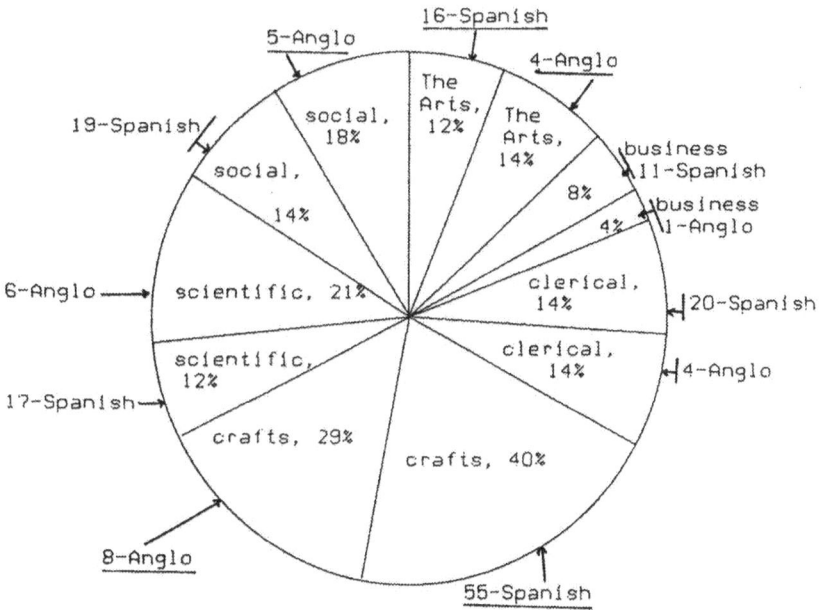

SPANISH/ANGLO
CAREER DECISION CATEGORIES

FEMALE/MALE

CAREER DECISION CATEGORIES

The pie graph shows the number of students, males and females and the percentage attaining high scores in the six career categories.

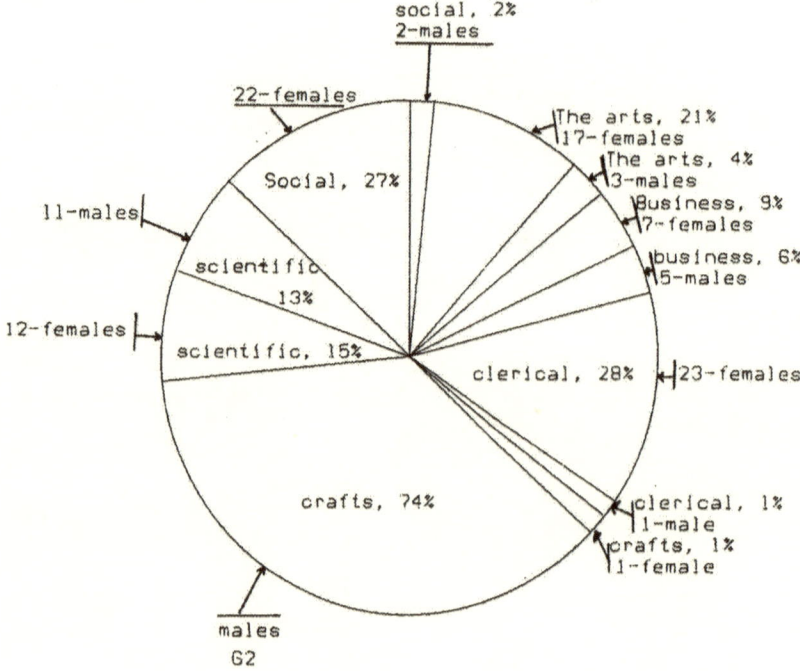

FEMALE/MALE
CAREER DECISION CATEGORIES

PERCENTAGE BREAKDOWN PER CATEGORY NUMBER OF STUDENTS WITH HIGH SCORES ETHNICITY AND SEX DIVISIONS

The pie graphs show the number of students and percentage per career categories of ethnicity and sex division of the students in the three year study.

PERCENTAGE BREAKDOWN PER CATEGORY
NUMBER OF STUDENTS-HIGH SCORES

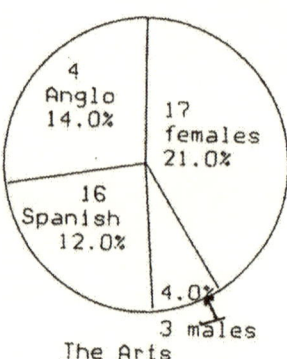

The Arts

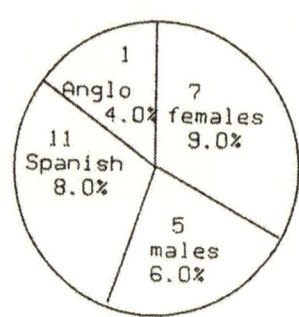

Business

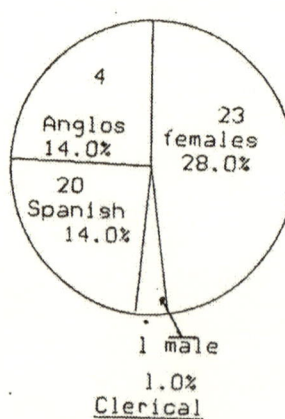

Clerical

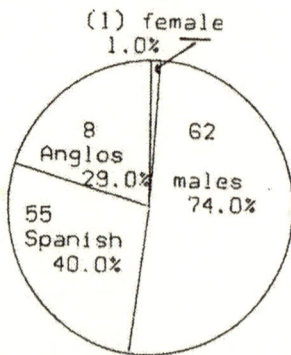

Crafts

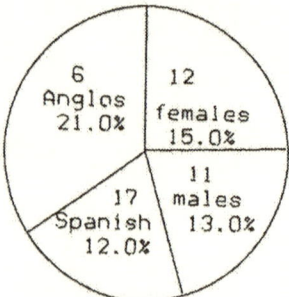

Scientific

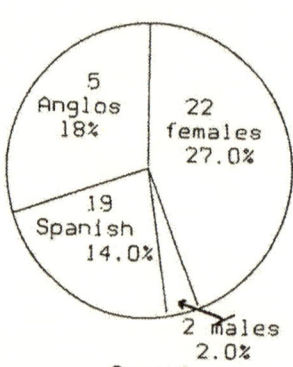

Social

36

NATIONAL ACHIEVEMENT PERCENTILE

THREE-YEAR COMPARISON PER CAREER SURVEYED

The bar graph shows the average achievement percentile attained for each group with highest scores in the six different career categories during the three years of the study. The bar graph shows the average of the total achievement percentile for the total group attained during each year of the study.

NATIONAL PERCENTILE
THREE-YEAR COMPARISON PER CAREER SURVEYED

THREE-YEAR COMPARISON CONTINUED

THREE-YEARS TOTAL
NAT'L PERCENTILE

THREE-YEAR' AVERAGES OF CTBS NATIONAL ACHIEVEMENT PERCENTILE

AND

CAREER INTEREST SURVEY STUDY OF STUDENTS' TOTAL NUMBER AND PERCENTAGE

The bar graph shows the average national achievement percentile for three years of the study for each group of students with high scores in the different career categories. The bar graph also shows the number of students with high scores in the different career categories.

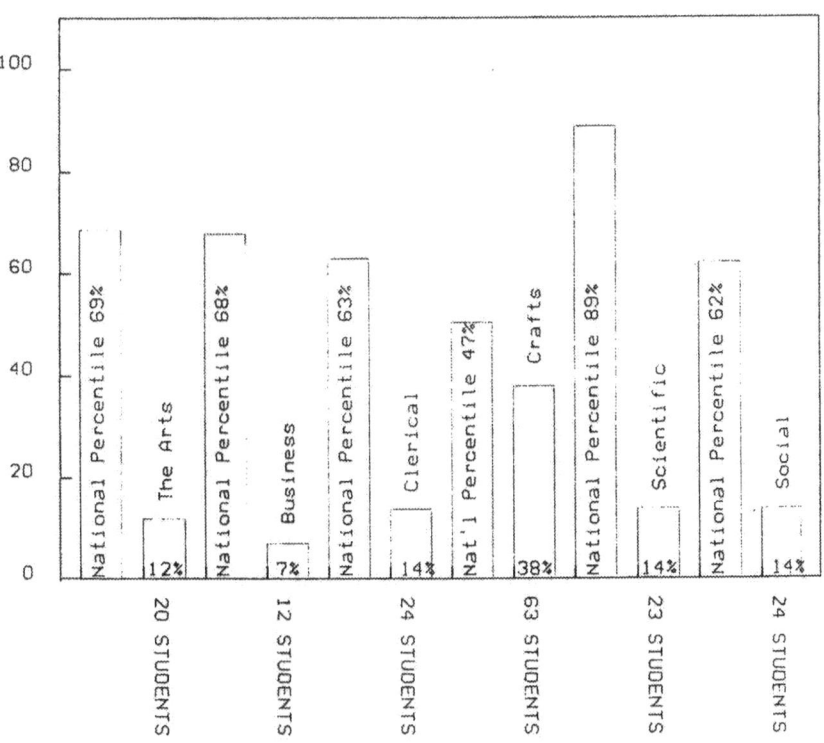

THREE YEARS' AVERAGES OF
CTBS NATIONAL PERCENTILE
AND
CAREER INTEREST SURVEY STUDY
STUDENTS TOTAL NUMBER/PERCENTAGE

SEX ORIENTATION PRESENTATION

Sex, that interesting term that scrutinizes our media, newspapers, radio, television, and controls a great portion of our conversation has been totally misconstrued in its meaning. It's loosely used by most means of communication, "They had sex last night," or "We had sex and. .." "With its true definition, no one can have sex. The term sex is defined in Webster's New Word Dictionary, as being "either of the two divisions, male and female, into which persons, animals, or plants are divided, with reference to their reproductive functions."

In group Sex Orientation presentations, the counselor is not going to change the existing definition of sex, nor is there any concern over its usage. Nevertheless, the true definition of sex may well serve as an opening to a Sex Orientation session, "Did you know that none of you can have sex?" (My understanding, "sex" according to definition, is knowing the difference between male and female; therefore, etc....)

Future references will be made later to the mentioned question. Of all group sessions the counselor holds throughout the school-year, possibly the sessions related to sex orientation taking into careful consideration specifics of sexual intercourse, is the session presented with greater contentious communicative patterns. Needs related to control of feelings and emotions carry greater possibilities of "misunderstandings" than most other sessions.

For a Sex Orientation session, the counselor should have clearance from the unit school principal. Furthermore, pending on the district's administrative population, the superintendent should be made aware of the intended session and his or her presence, as well as the unit principal should be re quested. Parents should always be notified about such sessions.

The school unit staff may request such sessions anytime throughout the school-year. The major Sex Orientation session is promoted for eighth-graders by the school counselor. This group is reaching a higher level of maturity related to their self and social feelings.

Furthermore, it's proposed that greater emotional experiences will be sustained. Awareness of self-protection related to self-responsibility are needs that are presented seeking to avoid future hardship for them.

As already stated, clearance for presentation has been granted from the administrative body. Parents are notified in writing of the Sex Orientation presentation. The parents' permission for their child's attendance is requested and so is their presence. The following is a sample of the format sent to the parents. Preferably, it should be signed by the school unit principal.

_____, 20_____

Parents of Eighth-Graders, (School unit's name)

(Date)_____ , (Counselor's name)___ , Counselor, will be providing a counseling session on Sex Orientation to the Eighth—Graders. Due to the increase of teenage pregnancies throughout the nation, (counselor's name) feels parents would profit by becoming aware of what the session has to offer. His/Her session is oriented toward the students learning about self- needs and understanding how to control self-behaviors. Otherwise, they should be aware and prepared to face the consequences. Parents are cordially invited to be present at this session.

I, _____, parent of_____ grant permission for my child to attend.

I, _____, parent of_____ do not grant permission for my child to attend.

I will attend:_____ I will not attend: _____

Respectfully,

Mr./Mrs./Ms_____,Principal

In general, Counselors' behavioral studies do not prepare them for laborious comprehension of biological explicit needs of sexual intercourse. Such explanation is best pro- vided by the expertise of doctors or nurses. The counselors are better trained in providing the psychological modes toward prevention of unwanted pregnancies.

Preparation for such a session, as already mentioned, carries the importance of becoming informed on technicalities related to sexual intercourse and its biological results. The definition of sex should be well understood. It is important for counselors to be acquainted with sex chromosomes. They should be prepared to explain at the session that the germ cell, the egg of the female and the germ cell of the male, the sperm, when joined, develop the creation of a child.

The Sex Orientation session in general will be attended by a number of parents. Expectation from those attending will vary, but positive results are expected. It is important that the counselor be well-prepared. Furthermore, regardless of feelings of tension experienced by the counselor, he/she must be prepared to promote a sincere "normal" approach to the normalcy of this emotion. Counselors who have the ability to initiate sincere humor will find such an approach to be a need that releases much tension.

After greetings, "I understand that at the age of thirteen you become teenagers. Some of you are already teenagers and some you will be in the near future. The question is: what's the big deal about being a teenager? (counselor listens to responses, if any) My understanding of a teenager is that at this age-level you are loaded with greater responsibility. I could be wrong, but I understand that as a teenager a major responsibility is to know the difference between being a male or a female. (counselor waits and listens for any humorous response)

Furthermore, I understand you now appreciate the companionship of the opposite sex. I think such appreciation is great! I'm sure you understand such responsibility also carries much accountability.

"Companionship with the opposite sex means you're experimenting with emotions between two human-beings. These emotions carry certain consequences if they are not carefully controlled. Emotions are mental states or conditions that satisfy feelings of desire in each one of us; for example: happiness, anger, sorrow, love and sex. (counselor gives examples of emotions)

"Having emotional needs is most normal. The results of these emotional needs that one feels are what produce the outcome of behaviors. Behaviors are those actions one ex presses verbally or physically because of an emotion one desires to fulfill. If the emotion one wishes to fulfill creates a scrupulous behavior that is not acceptable for whatever reason, then one must be prepared to suffer the consequences. (counselor gives examples: the emotion of desiring to punch someone, behavior-punching the someone, consequences, etc.)

"Understanding emotions, for example the desire to kiss, hug and touch, and then creating the behaviors of these emotions brings us to the reason for this sex-orientation session. Need for sex, just like food, water and sleep, is a natural feeling of human beings. Understand, all these needs, if overdone, will create consequences. Therefore, let me present to you my views on sex and love.

"Sex is defined in the dictionary as it being divided into two categories, being the male and female divisions of human beings, animals, plants and their reproductive functions. Therefore, no human beings can have sex. All human beings are already divided into a sex division of either being a male or female. (counselor listens to response, maybe check dictionary, etc..) Sex has also been defined as a natural feeling of human beings aroused or caused by emotions and satisfied by behaviors between a male and a female. This is the definition being used today for this session.

"Sex is a need and it's aroused from emotions. It's satisfied by kissing, touching and it will create greater need of satisfaction. If you don't control your feelings, then you're prepared to face the consequences. Having sexual intercourse means that at your age level or any age-level you're satisfying your emotions knowing the possibilities of what will follow from this behavior tomorrow.

"The consequences of not being able to control your feelings provide the possibility of getting pregnant. The biological explanation of pregnancy happens through sexual intercourse. The male's germ cell, the sperm, and female's germ cell, the egg, unite and a child is formed or created. That is possibly the greatest accomplishment that can ever happen to human beings; the creation of a child!

"Such unity of two humans, male and female, if they're ready to support a child's needs, cannot be matched. But if you're not ready with what's needed to support a child, then be extremely careful with your feelings. Learn to control them. Otherwise, be prepared to face a difficult period in your life.

"According to a local doctor, prenatal care and delivery of a child carries some expenses. Prenatal care means doctor checkups before delivery. Delivery means, of course, when you give birth to the child. For an uncomplicated prenatal care, if the teenager remains healthy all the time she's pregnant, the doctor's expenses will be approximately, $1,500.00. For an uncomplicated delivery, the expense for hospital services will be approximately $3,500.00.

"If the teenager has complications during her pregnancy, and she can't give normal birth, she will then need surgery to have the child delivered; that's called a cesarean or c-section. It would then increase the expense. Prenatal care for complicated pregnancies can run approximately from $1,500.00 to $2,000.00. For surgery, the cost would be approximately $2,200.00, and the hospital cost could be as much as $10,000.00.

"According to a study made, When Kids Have Babies, written in the Albuquerque Journal, by Daniel Q. Haney from the Associated Press, the youngest girls, ages 13 to 17 were 90% more likely to deliver prematurely than women in their early 20s. Furthermore, it points out that the leading cause of newborn deaths may be caused due to premature pregnancies. Accordingly, the study speculates that teenagers' bodies are still growing and therefore their bodies are competing with the unborn child for nutrients and premature births may be the results. (many other articles can be introduced)

"Many are the articles and texts written providing in formation related to protecting teenagers from becoming pregnant if they are not ready to face the many physical and mental needs that go with a pregnancy; read and learn, it's your life. You, as a teenager, must decide your future. If you're not ready to face what I have provided for you today, then learn to say, "No, I'm not ready."

"You young men, you can't get pregnant, but you can cause the hardships that I have mentioned for young ladies. I don't think it's much to be proud about. Will you stand up to your responsibilities, as a man should, if you and a girl created a pregnancy? You must face the facts; you're part of the reason for what she will face.

"Let me read you some of the comments from boys' reactions I've read and saved for this session: 'I was fourteen, she was sixteen, she should have known better-- My parents will be hurt, my Dad will kill me--I was fifteen and my father told me, sexual intercourse is for adults with responsibility, marry her. You need to pay the doctor, the hospital, rent a home, buy furniture, clothing, food, a car. You can create a child; be a man. Quit school, get a job and provide support like all men do. Get out! I was broke and Dad was no help; he was talking about thousands of dollars I didn't have--I saw the baby, I was a proud father and then they told me to get out; I never saw my son again, sometimes I cry. (responsibilities become realities, more can be added)

"The fact remains that you know yourself. All your behavioral actions are your responsibility. Don't believe the "I love you" scene constantly used. If they truly love you, they would respect you and not cause you potential hardship. Don't just say no, make the person that is saying that he truly loves you face what you may be facing. Ask him, "If I get pregnant, will you be there to support me with doctor and hospital expenses? Will you marry me?'

"Understand, there are other ways of preventing pregnancy, but such means are not proven to be 100% safe. Therefore, the only way of avoiding a pregnancy is for you to use your intelligence. Don't allow yourselves to be sexually aroused to the point where you can't stop. Learn and be prepared for those that promise promises that have no true support of your future.

"All that has been presented carries pleasure and depending on you, consequences. Possibly the greatest consequences that can happen from sexual intercourse is sexually transmitted diseases. The most dangerous one of the sexually transmitted diseases is AIDS, Acquired Immune Deficiency Syndrome.

"This disease can be transmitted from people that have the disease, either through sexual contact or through sharing of needles for drugs. So far, the disease, AIDS, has no cure and many thousands have died from having acquired this fatal disease.

"Other diseases that carry much danger if you're infected are gonorrhea and syphilis. These diseases are also transmitted. Gonorrhea can cause damage to your organs whereby women will no longer be able to have babies. Men will suffer much pain and his reproductive organs could also be damaged. Syphilis can cause heart disease, brain damage, blindness, and at times, death. (counselor mentions the fact that other STD exist and that the doctor or the nurse would have better information on them)

"Therefore, many are the consequences one faces in life due to the satisfaction of that emotion the body requires, sex. This is reality, and you can enjoy this very strong emotion of desire, but enjoy it with much caring for the person you are.

"Please answer all the ten questions in the questionnaire I'm presenting you. You don't have to turn it in to me or to anyone. You should know how you feel. I would recommend you share it with your parents."

QUESTIONS TO ASK YOURSELF

Teenagers can have sexual intercourse now, or they can wait. The decision is yours and it depends on your beliefs, your morals and your views of your future. (morals are those values learned from parents, clergymen, or others who care about you.)

1. Is having sex in agreement with my own moral values?
   yes_____ no_____
2. Would my parents approve of my having sex now?
   yes_____ no_____
3. Can I take full responsibility for my actions?
   yes_____ no_____
4. Am I willing to risk pregnancy, STD Sexually Transmitted Disease?
   yes_____ no_____
5. Am I prepared to inform my parents that I'm having a baby, or that I caused a girl to be with child?
   yes_____ no_____
6. If I have a child or if I cause a girl to have a child, am I responsible enough for its emotional, social and financial support?
   yes_____ no_____
7. Am I ready to pay the bills for prenatal care and hospital needs?
   yes_____ no_____
8. If the relationship breaks up, will I continue to care and support the child?
   yes_____ no_____
9. Can I handle the emotions of having the child to be placed for adoption?
   yes_____ no_____
10. Do I know better, and am I strong enough to control my emotions and behaviors by saying, "Not now, I'm not ready."?
   yes_____ no_____

"This session has been provided to make you aware of what you may be facing tomorrow. Furthermore, it has been provided to hopefully make you understand that neither your parents nor the counselor can stop you from doing as you wish with your future; it's you decision."

The Sex Orientation session is then opened for questions from the class participating and from the parents who have attended. Each class member is then presented with the following poster made for this occasion. Throughout the years this counselor provided counseling services; one pregnancy occurred among mid-high students.

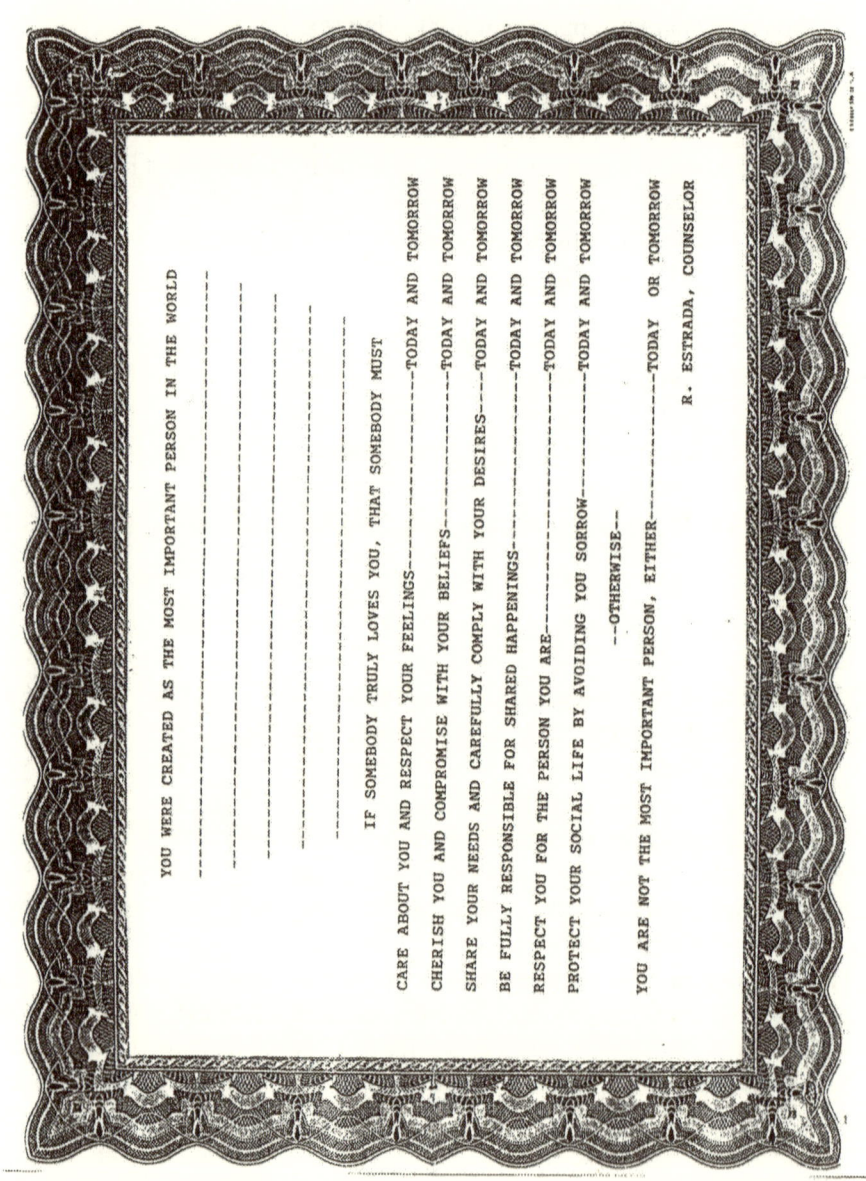

YOU WERE CREATED AS THE MOST IMPORTANT PERSON IN THE WORLD

IF SOMEBODY TRULY LOVES YOU, THAT SOMEBODY MUST

CARE ABOUT YOU AND RESPECT YOUR FEELINGS----------TODAY AND TOMORROW
CHERISH YOU AND COMPROMISE WITH YOUR BELIEFS----------TODAY AND TOMORROW
SHARE YOUR NEEDS AND CAREFULLY COMPLY WITH YOUR DESIRES-----TODAY AND TOMORROW
BE FULLY RESPONSIBLE FOR SHARED HAPPENINGS----------TODAY AND TOMORROW
RESPECT YOU FOR THE PERSON YOU ARE----------TODAY AND TOMORROW
PROTECT YOUR SOCIAL LIFE BY AVOIDING YOU SORROW----------TODAY AND TOMORROW
---OTHERWISE---

YOU ARE NOT THE MOST IMPORTANT PERSON, EITHER----------TODAY OR TOMORROW

R. ESTRADA, COUNSELOR

CAREER EDUCATION

Our educational system must hold the preparation of future employment as a priority. Therefore, the counselor's responsibilities extend to the preparation of future career awareness.

The intricate needs of future careers demand of the counselor the search and research that may instill in the minds of the student-population awareness of what education is designed to do. Students must become aware that schooling is a mandate seeking self-development and undertaking the need for enrichment of their skills for future expected employment.

Students must become aware that if they live to be 75 years of age, one-third, or 25 years of their lives, they must be committed to the life of work. With proper preparation these twenty-five years of their lives should become a challenge for their future survival.

Awareness of self-fulfillment needs in their careers' accomplishments should become a goal of their development. The work-world then becomes not survival for today but a challenging survival for tomorrow.

Enjoyment and regret are terminologies that students comprehend. For twenty-five years they are informed that they must prepare themselves to enjoy their work world. If they in the future, work only to exist and survive for today, and if they hate the work they are doing, can they imagine how much they are going to regret not preparing themselves for the "work-world?" At this early age, awareness of future preparation must be taken into careful consideration.

The work-world has different components, and the student population must become aware of such needs; therefore, they are informed that working is not only doing what they were hired to do. They must learn about communication skills, friendship, responsibility, self-awareness of potential and a desire of being successful at what they do. Thus the following Career Education Pattern is recommended:

The following filmstrips, which may no longer exist in their original development, were used from elementary to middle school level, grades 1st to 8th. (the following mentioned filmstrips may now be produced in video technology) These filmstrips were selected to promote awareness of self- development toward preparation of future careers.

The second semester of the school year, at the elementary level, three classes, first, third and fifth grades were shown the following filmstrips considered to promote major needs of career education. The first graders were shown the filmstrip: <u>Learning About Groups and Rules</u>.[11] The third graders the filmstrip, <u>Being Friends</u>,[12] and fifth graders the filmstrip, <u>Being Responsible</u>.[13]

Considering their age-levels, the counselor felt the student-population would gain greater maturity in their reasoning. Also, after six months of experiencing group interaction with each other, it would assist in setting the scene for the filmstrips' topics.

The first-graders are made aware of the need to learn how live with others. Furthermore, they are informed that once they start school, it's important to learn how to live with others because that's going to happen for the rest of their lives. They become aware of this life-pattern fact. The family, future schooling, and the work-world, are examples of the need to learn about self-actions that will be needed throughout their lives.

The third-graders learn about needs of awareness in making friends in new social environments. Furthermore, they learn about accepting those who may be new in their own environments. The filmstrip assists in providing the need to understand interactions of behaviors that they will face in the future.

The fifth-graders learn through the filmstrip of the needs for responsibilities. It promotes the awareness of being concerned over self-actions in relation to the needs of others. Learning to share is a major factor of the filmstrip. Furthermore, it promotes the concept that responsibility is a need of today and not a need that can wait until tomorrow.

The filmstrips for the elementary students promote much awareness of self and social needs toward self-development for future expected careers. The counselor's responsibility is to relate these mentioned needs to concerns facing the work world today. Awareness of these self and social needs is preparation for learning about work expectations existing today and a need for tomorrow. Furthermore, the elementary student population is prepared for greater understanding of needed preparation of the work-world at the middle school.

At the middle school, grades sixth, seventh and eighth the career pattern changes to more specific directions on the world of work. Their age level, preparation for high school, and future views of work expectations are introduced. The following filmstrips were used to promote these mentioned needs:

Sixth graders are informed that they are not elementary children anymore. Therefore, they must become more mature in preparing for the future. The filmstrip, Where Will I fit In? is a filmstrip that relates to their age-level. It promotes in its content the needed understanding of what is work? It follows showing the students' differences in a number of careers: school, government, and construction.

The seventh graders are made aware they will never be elementary children anymore. Furthermore, they are made aware that they have the responsibility of preparing them selves for leadership as eighth graders. Also, in high school, it's their responsibility to begin to prepare for a future career.

The filmstrip, You Can Be Anything,[15] strongly reinforces this needed concept. The filmstrip promotes a need for looking at tomorrow and the psychological view of being what you desire to be, pending on your self-potential. The filmstrip promotes the understanding that the world is wide open, and boys and girls can do anything.

The counselor reinforces these concepts with the understanding that they must become aware of their own self-abilities. Awareness is made that at their present age-level; they have one more year before reaching the high-school level and approximately five-years before they will be joining the adult world. Therefore, a major responsibility to be part of that adult world is to be prepared for a future career.

Much emphasis on career education is placed for the eight graders. They are approached and treated as young adults preparing for high school and in a matter of four years, the world of work.

During the first session on career education, they are grouped and presented with a listing of Job Profiles, a list of the Twenty Fastest Growing Occupations plus the Twenty Fastest Declining Occupations. This information may be available at an employment office.

Discussion promotes the reason for these listings, their present age-level and the up-coming stage of their education in high school. Groups of four of five eighth graders, as they were divided, are prompted to hold discussions in relation to future careers that they may be interested in for future careers' preparation. They are told that they are to select no less than five careers that they feel they may someday be interested in for future employment.

Motivation, in general, is found to be strongly developed. They are informed they will be taking a Career Decision System Survey at a later date that will give them a good view of their abilities in relation to their present self-analysis of careers they desire.

During this session, they are provided with the following form which is to be compared with the Career Decision System Survey they will be taking; therefore, copies are made of the form and it's saved for future use.

STUDENT'S NAME_____ GRADE LEVEL_____
___ YEAR_____

PRE-CHOSEN FUTURE CAREERS

20___ Future ninth-graders, fill the below blanks showing no less than five future employment careers you would like to prepare yourself during the next four years of high school.

1. You have job profiles before you showing future careers with brief explanations of what each career entails. You may use this information to determine your wishes for a future career.
2. You have information showing the twenty fastest growing and the twenty most declining occupations. You may, if you wish, use this information to determine you future career desires.

FUTURE NINTH GRADERS: It's important you do the best you can in choosing the following five possible careers that you may someday hold. (be aware, you will be taking a Career Decision Survey that will give you a good view of abilities you presently have. You will then be able to compare your present selection of careers with your present abilities as the survey will show)

ASK QUESTIONS IF YOU NEED ASSISTANCE --------------------------------------
1st career choice_____
2nd Career choice_____
3rd Career choice_____
4th Career choice_____
5th Career choice_____

You have now compiled career interests as the eighth graders have voluntarily stated. The next session with them will be the administering of the Career Decision—Making System. The time for administering this Career System and comparative analysis with the career pre-chosen format is approximately 45 to 60 minutes.

Level I of the Career Decision-Making System is a hand scored booklet. It is self- descriptive and directions are easy to follow. The survey has 96 career items to be completed and shows results for six career areas, Crafts, Scientific, The Arts, Social, Business and Office Operation. Description of each of these careers is provided.

The Job Chart for each of the career carries much information related to needs of future career preparation. Based on high scores attained for any of the careers mentioned, the eighth-graders learn what the needs are for each of the particular careers. The chart shows typical jobs showing whether they require manual, skilled crafts or technical needs. It provides the schools subjects that should be concentrated on, the job values and abilities needed for each specific career. A description of each one of these functions is provided.

The final section of the Career Decision-Making booklet provides a summary. The summary promotes a view for the students of their present career interests. It requests of them to list what they consider their best subjects, career values they find important at the present and abilities they feel they hold.

After the Career Decision-Making System implementation, the students then compare results with their previous pre-chosen future careers format. Results of these comparisons are most interesting. To some they find it most gratifying, and to others much disappointment. Nevertheless, the objective of the career sessions, this counselor feels has been well achieved. The students are very much aware that preparation for future careers is a priority as they continue to strive toward future self-development.

It's recommended that an evening session with parents and their eighth grade son or daughter should be held. Attendance of this career-education session has been experienced to be well- attended. Therefore, the following memorandum is provided as an example:

MEMORANDUM

TO:	Parents and eighth-graders
SUBJECT:	Career Education Project Explanation
FROM:	Counselor
DATE:	_____

Eighth-graders have finished a series of career education sessions considered needed for high school preparation and for their own self-development. Many are the positive and negative behavioral impacts in our national society today; therefore, this career education project has been designed to assist them in learning about self-fulfillment and awareness of need in preparing themselves for the work-world tomorrow.

Please do your utmost to attend. The career education project will be discussed in detail. Therefore, this session is to be held to support your son or daughter as they prepare themselves for tomorrow. Furthermore, the session is intended to inform you of needed support for your child's progress for future preparation of self-development.

The session will be held at: _____ at _____ etc.

The parent session is held. Parents are informed of the total process taken, starting with the filmstrip and proceeding with the sessions held. They are informed that the career project was intended toward awareness of self- fulfillment of their child seeking to identify their interests, skills, and values as they explored future careers.

During this session, parental grouping is recommended with their child also being part of the group. Parents are made aware that the careers' results they are viewing does not necessarily mean that the child must continue to prepare only for those particular careers. Greater preparation in high school and other agencies may develop greater knowledge of self and social skills that may lead to other careers.

As parental discussion develops within the groups they are provided with the following questionnaire:

1. Do you and your child feel that the careers recommended by the process taken relate to your child's abilities?
2. Do you feel that your child's personality relates to the careers' requirements in skills and values?
3. Will your child in the future be able to cope with the work-habits of any of the careers that have shown some of his or her abilities?

4. Do you feel the present careers you are viewing will have future training expectations and will your child be able to cope with these expectations?
5. Do you and your child feel this career education project will assist your child to be more aware of future needs?

After questions and answers, the counselor recommends future guidance. The group is made aware that the academical efforts of public education have as a major priority preparation for future employment. The parents are provided with a format to evaluate the career decision-making project as presented:

CAREER DECISION MAKING SYSTEM

Date: _____

School unit: _____

Parental evaluation or presentation: (Counselor's name)

1. _____ I felt I learned more about my child's career abilities.
2. _____ I didn't learn anything that I didn't know about my child's career abilities.
3. _____ I understood all that was presented by the counselor.
4. _____ I understood some of what was presented by the counselor.
5. _____ I didn't understand anything that was presented by the counselor.
6. _____ I felt the bilingual presentation (if available) was needed.
7. _____ I felt the bilingual presentation was not needed.
8. _____ I felt enough time was provided for the presentation.
9. _____ I felt we needed more time for the presentation.
10. _____ I feel the Career Decision—Making System project will help my child.
11. _____ I feel the Career Decision-Making System will not help my child.
12. _____ I feel such services are needed to prepare students for the future.
13. _____ I feel such services are not needed to prepare students for the future.

I consider the Career project: good   fair   poor
I consider the presentation: good   fair   poor
Comments, if any: _____

_____

_____

_____

Signature, if you wish_____
Gracias!

QUICK TEMPER

The child that is referred due to behaviors promoting vocal or physical reactions for minor infractions usually claims such actions are caused because of having a quick temper. For such a referral, the counselor should have a copy of the child's standardized tests.

If the standardized test shows the child has average or above-average academical potential, then the following counseling procedure has proven successful. The individualized session proceeds with the counselee being a young girl.

"According to this referral, the reason you're meeting with me is because you are getting into trouble constantly. What's causing you to consistently behave the way you're be having?"

"I don't know. I guess it's because I have a quick temper and I act wrong right away. I guess that's why."

"I suppose that's why it's happening; a quick temper. I'm sort of lost. What's a quick temper?"

"Well, you know, I get angry right away and I either say something that I shouldn't, or maybe even try to slap those that bother me."

"I see, so that's a quick temper. What causes a quick temper?"

"I don't know. All I know is that I have a quick temper. I can't help it; it's just that I get angry right away.

"I guess not everyone has a quick temper. What do you think? Do you think everyone has a quick temper?"

"No, not everyone, I do."

"I'm glad not everyone has a quick temper. Can you imagine how it would be? Everyone would be jumping at each others' throats for minor negative actions."

"Yes, that would be terrible, I guess."

"Tell me, do you think people are born with quick tempers?

"I don't know, I guess I was, because I have one."

"From what I have studied and read, no one is born with a quick temper. From what I understand, as you grow older, you develop the habit of having a quick temper. Do you think you have developed such a habit?"

"No, I didn't develop it; I have always had a quick tem per."

"Even when you were a baby, do you recall, or have you been told that you had a quick temper?"

"My mom says if I was hungry or wet or anything I didn't care for, I would scream."

"I see. You see, as a baby you were developing the habit of having a quick temper. You were hungry, you screamed, you were wet, you screamed; you wanted to be held, you screamed. Today, if things are not as you wish them to be, you don't scream anymore, but you react with a negative approach."

"Maybe you're right, but I'm older now; I wish I could control my temper and not act so quickly to things I don't like."

"Maybe I can help you, but the decision to get rid of a quick temper is totally up to you."

"I'll listen, but it's not easy to get rid of a quick temper, I know; I've tried."

"All habits are hard to break, but let's see what we can do to break this one that is messing you up. Are you with me in trying?"

"I'll try."

"You see this standardized test that shows your abilities in school. The results show that you're average in some areas and above-average in others. (the counselee is shown results) This tells me you have good mental abilities. The reason we're looking at these results is because if you didn't have the mental abilities that you have, then you would have an excuse for acting up with a quick temper."

"I don't quite understand, what do you mean?"

"Let me put it this way. If my mental abilities were below average, and I didn't know how to get results, then I would explode with anger. I would try to accomplish what I felt I needed by showing anger, or what you call a quick temper. It could well be understood that I didn't know any better. That, young lady, is not your case; you know better."

"I see what you're saying, but I do have the habit; I know I do."

"The habit is still there, I know. Look at yourself, what would you consider more important? The way your classmates are looking at you now, or a new you that is liked for showing good feelings for others? Young lady, the decision is yours, and I know which way you're going. With your mental abilities you know that self-development calls for the need to be appreciated. You want to be appreciated; you decide; the quick temper habit must go."

"I know you're right, I'll let you know how the new me makes out; thanks."

Such individualized session, researching the child's home life, and re-affirming the concept that quick tempers are developed, promotes for the counselor the avenues of future direction. The concept of average and above average mental abilities is a strong reinforcement to assist the child to determine the needed behavioral factors to break the habit of quick tempers.

THE BOXER

The child referred for constant fighting needs to learn about himself or herself. The responses for fighting are many. The counselor listens and mostly agrees with the counselee. The following stated approach is an example of a fighting young boy.

"You're referred for fighting. According to this referral, this is not the first time. What's happening in your life?"

"I don't know."

"Come on, you must know. You're doing the fighting. You're not fighting just for the fun of fighting, are you?"

"Well, no, but they bug me and I get angry and hit them."

"What do they do that bugs you?"

"They call me names and sometimes they push me."

"They must be bugging and pushing you all the time; you seem to be fighting constantly."

"Yes they are, and I hate it."

"You have to understand; I bet you're not the only one that is being called names and pushed. You know how young people your age act. The others don't seem to be fighting because they are called names or because they are pushed."

"They make me angry and I'm not going to take it."

"Sometimes I guess I won't take it either, but I find that you're hurting yourself with your actions. You're the one who's in trouble. The rest are out there enjoying themselves. Maybe you're trying to prove you're pretty tough?"

"I can beat them up. They are not going to mess with me.

"If you really need to defend yourself, I guess fighting is alright. I don't think that's the case with you. You're fighting, but for what reason? You don't see the others fighting and they are facing the same things you are."

"I told you, I get angry."

"I know you said that, but do you think you're winning when you fight?"

"I sure do, they're not going to beat me up."

"Let's see, you knock the guy down, you give him a black eye or a bloody nose; therefore, you win the fight, right?"

"Yup, I told you, I don't lose any fights."

"I guess you're right; you won your fights. I wonder how many friends you have lost because they don't like you beating up others. I wonder how much the teachers respect you because you beat others. Sometimes winning a fight means you end up losing much for yourself, friends and respect, don't you think so?"

"I guess so. I guess I better do something to stop fighting."

"Do you understand that sometimes winning is losing?"

"Yea, I guess so. I hadn't realized it, but the way you put it, I guess I'm losing, right?"

"You see, when you fight you're putting on a show for people. They'll tell you how tough you are so that you will continue to put up free shows. In many instances they're clapping when you fight, but behind your back, they may be laughing at you. They're using you and it doesn't cost them a cent. You're the only one losing. Do you understand?"

"I guess so."

"Look, you've proven you're pretty tough. Why don't you train yourself to be a boxer someday? If you do, then you will be putting up a show for money, and I mean money. Do you know how much money a boxer makes?"

"Yea, they make millions, I guess."

"They sure do, so will you someday if you train your self. It's something to think about. From now on think before you punch somebody. Count to ten slowly and think of what you will be able to do someday for a money-making show that takes only a few minutes. You're no fool, you're tough and smart enough to know better."

"What about the name calling; what do I do? It makes me angry."

"I told you that you're smart, use your smartness, simply ask the person who is calling you names, 'Why are you calling me those names? I don't like them. Why do you do it? You will find out that they probably don't really know why they are doing it, and I bet they will stop doing it."

"I'm going to try it, but I'm not chicken. I'm not afraid of them."

"Do you know it takes guts to prove that you're not chicken? It takes guts and smartness to walk away from a fight. You happen to have both of them, guts and smartness; therefore, you're no chicken."

"I guess not. I'm going to try."

"You let me know how things turn out. Who knows, maybe one of these days I'll be paying to see you fight, you could be one heck of a boxer."

This approach has been proven successful toward motivating positive future needs; yet, promoting awareness of negative present behaviors. The counselor should check into the child's family background. In many instances this type of child comes from families where physical displays are the answers to accomplishments.

If this is the case, and the child continues to fight, then it's recommended that a parent session be called. In most cases, a session such as the one used for the example is all that's needed.

THE CARROT THEORY

It's extremely important that the counselor keep open communication at all times with the staff. The counselor needs to be informed on the classes' abilities and capabilities. For those students that are doing below average class work, the counselor needs to know why. Are such students doing below average work because of lack of effort, or due to the fact that they are not capable of achievement due to mental potential?

If the students are doing below average class work due to lack of effort, and their standardized tests show the students could be doing better in achievement, they might be ready for the presentation of The Carrot Theory.

The Carrot Theory was designed seeking a humorous comparative approach toward self-development and growth. Such a theory has proven successful particularly for students in the intermediate schooling stage at the elementary level. This counseling presentation can be presented either in a group-counseling session or also for individualized sessions.

All counselors can draw a carrot on the chalkboard. The following pages to this section on the Carrot Theory show a drawing of a carrot and a student. Ask the students not to laugh and inform them you're an artist. Once your drawing appears, the presentation starts:

"According to your teacher, none of you belong here with below average grades. Also, according to this standardized testing records I'm seeing you sure don't belong here! I'm wondering; Why are you here? What excuses can you give me for having made below-average grades these nine-weeks? (counselor listens to excuses)

"I want you to understand you're not primary children anymore; therefore, I'm sure you understand the need that with physical growth, responsibility must also grow. You're already a fourth-grader, and your standing in life and in school has also advanced. Understand, as you grow physically and as you advance yourselves in life, you must advance your responsibilities by putting in some true effort to develop your mental abilities. If you're not careful, your brain might dry out!

"Let me show you. I want you to look at this beautiful picture I have drawn of you and a carrot. Don't laugh; that's you standing by the carrot. A seed was planted and the carrot started to grow. It grew daily, and when you watered it and hoed the weeds around it, growth could easily be observed. It grew so much it burst out of the land level. That growing is what we call physical growth; it can be seen by everybody.

"Look at your physical growth, just like the carrot; it's amazing! From last year to today, everybody can see how much you have grown. Just like the carrot, there is nothing you can do about physical growth; it will be there till you finally stop growing.

"The carrot will grow and will probably end up in a salad bowl. That's what vegetables are for, right? What about you? Look at your physical growth; are you headed for the salad bowl? (counselor listens to responses) The difference here is that the carrot produces physical growth, but the carrot does not have a brain; you do. At least I hope you do!

"You will grow physically, you will get older, and as you continue to develop, you must also develop the growth of your brain. Otherwise, you might end up in the salad bowl.

"You're no carrot, so wake up; you must develop your mental abilities to match your physical growth and the stage you have reached in life. Understand, we cannot see your mental growth; therefore, you have to prove that your mind is developing. This proof of mental development is proven when you no longer are students with below-average grades on your report cards.

"You understand what I'm telling you? Alright, next time we meet, I want you to tell me if you're heading for the salad bowl to join the carrot, or to eat what's in the salad bowl! It's up to you we'll meet again in three weeks. (questions)

Results have been most positive and for some reason, this "comparative carrot and self analysis" has improved effort in grades' achievement extensively.

COUNSELING FORMS

The following counseling forms were developed from study and experience of services provided. The major impact of counseling services followed this directional pattern: Individualized staff referrals, Group counseling sessions, and Parental counseling requests.

1. The Individualized Referral Form was used for staff referrals of students they felt needed counseling services.

2. The Counselor Follow-up Form was used to provide the final report to the staff member who promoted the referral.

3. The Group Counseling Request Form was used for requests of group counseling services, either classes or specific groups. It was requested of staff members to provide their requests no less than a week in advance for needed counselor's preparation time. The Form provides for immediate evaluation of the group counseling presentation. The staff member requesting the group counseling services and others if present, were asked for such an evaluation.

4. The Parent (s) Counseling Services Form was structured bilingually, English and Spanish. After conclusion of the counseling sessions with the child referred, the form was returned to the parent (s).

5. The Student Counseling Reference Form assisted in keeping a record of those students that were meeting with the counselor. The request on the form for brothers or sisters and whether they were younger or older provided for the counselor avenues of reasons to be used for improvement. If brothers or sisters were younger, than the referred student found him/herself in need of setting an example. If they were older, the referred student found him/herself in need of possibly trying to accomplish whatever level of success his/her older siblings had already achieved.

INDIVIDUALIZED REFERRAL FORM

Student's name: _____ Grade level _____ Age_____

Staff-member referring _____ Date _____

CHECK, IF ANY OF THE BELOW, APPLY:
A. _____ Seems to have personal emotional problems with appear to be affecting his/her academic progress.
B. _____ Seems to have personal emotional problems which appear to be affecting his/her social adjustment.
C. _____ Seems to be in need of psychological help.
D. _____ Seems to be in need of remedial help in his/her studies.
E. _____ Has become a discipline problem.
F. _____ Lacks personal cleanliness and neatness.
G. _____ School attendance is poor.

CHECK PROPER BLANKS BELOW, COMMENT (5) IF DESIRED.
HOW EFFECTIVE IS THIS STUDENT IN/WITH: COMMENT(S)

ATTITUDE	good _____	fair _____	poor _____
CLASS WORK EFFORT	good _____	fair _____	poor _____
TEACHER COMMUNICATION	good _____	fair _____	poor _____
CLASSMATES PARTICIPATION	good _____	fair _____	poor _____
PARTICIPATION	good _____	fair _____	poor _____
ASSIGNMENT COMPLIANCE	good _____	fair _____	poor _____
MAKE-UP WORK	good _____	fair _____	poor _____

IN DETAIL, STATE YOUR REASON(S) FOR REFERRAL: _____
_____
_____
_____
_____
_____

SPECIFIC BEHAVIORAL PATTERNS NOTICED: _____
_____
_____
_____
_____
_____

Rural Counseling Services

COUNSELOR'S FOLLOW-UP FORM

STUDENT'S NAME _____ GRADE LEVEL_____ DATE_____
REFERRED BY:_____
STUDENT MET WITH COUNSELOR—
        DATE _____ TOTAL SESSIONS_____

COMMENTARY SECTION--RESULTS/RECOMMENDATION(S): _____

_____
_____
_____
_____
_____
_____
_____
_____
_____
_____
_____
_____
_____
_____
_____
_____
_____
_____
_____
_____
_____
_____
_____
_____
_____
_____
_____
_____
_____
_____
_____

SUBMITTED TO: (1) _____ (2) _____
                DATE:_____ DATE: _____

GROUP COUNSELING REQUEST SESSION

DATE OF REQUEST: _____ SCHOOL UNIT: _____

STAFF-MEMBER(S) REQUESTING:_____

GRADE-LEVEL OR SPECIFIC GROUP:_____

GROUP COUNSELING TOPIC TO BE PRESENTED: _____

_____

REQUESTED DATE OF PRESENTATION: _____ TIME:_____

CHECK ONE FOR PRESENTATION EVALUATION:

1.   GOOD_____   2. FAIR_____   3. POOR_____

CHECK ONE, YOUR VIEWS, ON GROUP COMPREHENSION OF
PRESENTATION

1.   GOOD_____   2. FAIR_____   3. POOR

STAFF AND OTHERS PRESENT, COMMENTS:_____

_____

_____

_____

GRACIAS

COUNSELOR' S VIEWS/REACTIONS: _____

_____

_____

_____

_____

_____

_____

_____

_____

_____

_____

Rural Counseling Services

PARENT(S) COUNSELING SERVICES FORM FORMA
PATERNAL DE SOLICITUD PARA EL CONSEJERO

PARENT(S)   DATE
PADRES _____   FECHA: _____

COMMUNITY   SCHOOL UNIT
COMUNIDAD _____UNIDAD I ESCUELA

STUDENT   AGE   GRADE
STUDIANTE _____   EDAD_____   GRADO_____

CONCERN/ PRO BLEM
CONCERNIR/PROBLEMA_____
_____
_____
_____
_____
_____
_____
_____
_____

COUNSELOR'S VIEW(S) PUNTO DE VISTA DEL CONSEJERO

DATE
FECHA_____. _____, _____, _____
_____
_____
_____
_____
_____

SUBMITTED TO/SOMETIDO PARA: _____

DATE/FECHA: _____, _____, _____

STUDENT COUNSELING REFERENCE FORM

Student's Name: _____

            Age _____ Grade Level _____

Parent(s): _____

Purpose of session: _____ Date: _____

Community/Address:_____

Telephone number:_____

Brother(s) _____Younger _____ Older_____

Sister(s) _____Younger _____ Older_____

STUDENT COUNSELING REFERENCE FORM

Student's Name: _____

            Age _____ Grade Level _____

Parent(s): _____

Purpose of session: _____ Date: _____

Community/Address:_____

Telephone number:_____

Brother(s) _____Younger _____ Older_____

Sister(s) _____Younger _____ Older_____

STUDENT COUNSELING REFERENCE FORM

Student's Name: _____

            Age _____ Grade Level _____

Parent(s): _____

Purpose of session: _____ Date: _____

Community/Address:_____

Telephone number:_____

Brother(s) _____Younger _____ Older_____

Sister(s) _____Younger _____ Older_____

BIBLIOGRAPHY

(1)   Maslow, Abraham H., Toward a Psychology of Being. D. Van Nostrand Company, Inc., New York, NY 10003, Copyright 1962. (Introduction)

(2)   Beck, Canton E., Philosophical Foundations of Guidance. Prentice-Hall, Inc., 200 Old Tappan Road, Old Tappan, New Jersey 07675, Copyright 1963. (The Supernatural Power, P. 2)

(3)   Blocher, Donald H., Developmental Counseling. John Wiley & Sons, 605 3rd. Avenue, New York, MY 10158, Copyright 1966, 1974. (Leadership Stages of Life, P. 1)

(4)   Allport, Gordon W., Becoming. Yale University Press, P.O Box 209040, New Haven, Connecticut 06520, Copy right 1955, 1968. (Judgement Theory, P. 1)

(5)   Darley, John M., Glucksberg, Sam, Kamin, Leon J., Kinchla, Ronald A., Psychology. Prentice hail, Inc., 200 Old Tappan Road, Old Tappan, New Jersey 07675. Copy right 1981. (Study Habit Formation Theory, P. 1)

(6)   "Definition" Webster New Word Dictionary. Dictionary Editorial Offices: New World Dictionaries, 850 Euclid Avenue, Cleveland, Ohio 44114, Copyright Simon & Schuster, Inc., Copyright 1986. (Success Theory, P. 1) & (Sex Orientation, P. 1)

(7)   Comprehensive Tests of Basic Skills, Form U and V Norms Books, Grades 7-12. The McGraw—Hill Companies, Inc., 20 Ryan Ranch Road, Monterey, California 93940—5703, copyright 1985—87. (Three—Year Study, P. 1)

(8)   Comprehensive Tests of Basic Skills Preliminary Report, The McGraw-Hill Companies, Inc., 20 Ryan Ranch Road, Monterey, California 93940—5703, copyright 1985—87. (Three—Year Study, P. 1)

(9)   Harrington, Thomas F. PhD., O'Shea, Arthur J. PhD., Career Decision-Making System Revised. American Guidance Service, 4201 Woodland

Road, Circle Pines, Minnesota 55014—1796, copyright 1992—1994, (Same page as number 8 above, P. 1)

(10)   Haney, Daniel Q., "Age, Not Poverty, Blamed for Infant Deaths When Teens Have Babies." Lang, T. H. Publisher, <u>Albuquerque Journal,</u> Journal Center, 7777 Jefferson NE, Albuquerque, New Mexico 87109-4343, Copyright 1926. (Sex Orientation, P. 8)

(11)   Filmstrips, <u>Learning About Groups and Rules</u>. Hanna Barbara Prod. Inc., Copyright 1982. (Career Education, P. 2)

(12)   Filmstrips, <u>Being Friends.</u> Random House School Division, 400 Hahn Road, Westminster, Maryland 21157, copyright 1981. (Career Education, P. 2)

(13)   Filmstrips, <u>Being Responsible</u>. Random House School Divi sion, 400 Hahn Road, Westminster, Maryland 21157, copy right 1979. (Career Education, P. 2)

(14)   Filmstrips, <u>Where Will I Fit In?</u> Random House School Division, 400 Bennett Cerf Drive, Westminster, Maryland 21157, Copyright 1971. (Career Education, P. 5)

(15)   Filmstrips, <u>You Can Be Anything</u>. Random House School Division, 400 Hahn Road, Westminster, Maryland 21157, copyright 1975. (Career Education, P. 5)

ABOUT THE AUTHOR

The author attained a B.A. degree from Highlands University, an M.A. degree from the University of Santa Clara, and a an Ed.S degree from the University of New Mexico. In his 26 years of educational services, he served as an elementary, mid high and high school teacher, and also served as school principal and Director of Instruction in all three levels of public education. In all three levels of public education he also served as counselor. He taught college courses as a professor substitute and taught college courses on an extension basis. Furthermore, he was a candidate of the Fellowship Program and later a Consultant for Ford Foundation.